olive

101 BRILLIANT BAKING IDEAS

1 3 5 7 9 10 8 6 4 2

Published in 2009 by BBC Books, an imprint of Ebury Publishing
A Random House Group company.

Recipes © BBC Magazines 2009
Photographs © BBC Magazines 2009
Book design © Woodlands Books 2009
All recipes contained within this book first appeared in BBC **olive** magazine

The Random House Group Limited Reg. No. 954009

Addresses for companies within the Random House Group can be found at
www.randomhouse.co.uk

A CIP catalogue record for this book is available from the British Library.

The Random House Group Limited supports The Forest Stewardship Council (FSC), the
leading international forest certification organization. All our titles that are printed on
Greenpeace approved FSC certified paper carry the FSC logo. Our paper procurement
policy can be found at www.rbooks.co.uk/environment

To buy books by your favourite authors and register for offers visit www.rbooks.co.uk

Printed and bound by Firmengruppe APPL, aprinta druck, Wemding, Germany
Colour origination by Dot Gradations Ltd, UK

Commissioning Editor: Muna Reyal
Project Editor: Laura Higginson
Designer: Kathryn Gammon
Production: Lucy Harrison
Picture Researcher: Gabby Harrington

ISBN: 978 184 607812 5

olive

101 BRILLIANT BAKING IDEAS

Editor
Janine Ratcliffe

BOOKS

Contents

Introduction 6

Big cakes 10

Biscuits, cookies and brownies 72

Essex County Council Libraries

Introduction

Everyone loves a slice of homemade cake or a muffin still warm from the oven. Whether you've got a special occasion to celebrate or you just fancy whipping up a batch of biscuits, you'll find everything you need in this new collection of brilliant baking recipes.

There are recipes here for every level of cook, and if time is precious you won't have to spend all day in the kitchen either. As well as some more challenging cakes for keen cooks there are plenty of easy, quick recipes for more instant gratification too.

The **olive** team have hand picked their all-time favourite sweet treats for this collection – gorgeous recipes like *Fluffy coconut and lime cake* (pictured opposite, see page 36 for the recipe).

As always, all the recipes have been thoroughly tested in the **olive** kitchen to make sure they taste fabulous and work for you first time. So grab your apron and get cooking – baking is back!

Janine Ratcliffe

Janine Ratcliffe
Food Editor
olive magazine

Notes and Conversions

NOTES ON THE RECIPES

• Where possible, we use humanely reared meats, free-range chickens and eggs, and unrefined sugar.

• Eggs are large unless stated otherwise. Pregnant women, elderly people, babies and toddlers, and anyone who is unwell should avoid eating raw and partially cooked eggs.

APPROXIMATE WEIGHT CONVERSIONS

• All the recipes in this book are listed with metric measurements.

• Cup measurements, which are used by cooks in Australia and America, have not been listed here as they vary from ingredient to ingredient. Please use kitchen scales to measure dry/solid ingredients.

OVEN TEMPERATURES

gas	°C	fan °C	°F	description
¼	110	90	225	Very cool
½	120	100	250	Very cool
1	140	120	275	Cool or slow
2	150	130	300	Cool or slow
3	160	140	325	Warm
4	180	160	350	Moderate
5	190	170	375	Moderately hot
6	200	180	400	Fairly hot
7	220	200	425	Hot
8	230	210	450	Very hot
9	240	220	475	Very hot

SPOON MEASURES

Spoon measurements are level unless otherwise specified.

• 1 teaspoon (tsp) = 5ml
• 1 tablespoon (tbsp) = 15ml
• 1 Australian tablespoon = 20ml (cooks in Australia should measure 3 teaspoons where 1 tablespoon is specified in a recipe)

APPROXIMATE LIQUID CONVERSIONS

metric	imperial	US
60ml	2fl oz	$\frac{1}{4}$ cup
125ml	4fl oz	$\frac{1}{2}$ cup
175ml	6fl oz	$\frac{3}{4}$ cup
225ml	8fl oz	1 cup
300ml	10fl oz/$\frac{1}{2}$ pint	1$\frac{1}{4}$ cups
450ml	16fl oz	2 cups/1 pint
600ml	20fl oz/1 pint	2$\frac{1}{2}$ cups
1 litre	35fl oz/1$\frac{3}{4}$ pints	1 quart

Please note that an Australian cup is 250ml, $\frac{3}{4}$ cup is 190ml, $\frac{1}{2}$ cup is 125ml, $\frac{1}{4}$ cup is 60ml.

Chocolate and cardamom torte

40 minutes ■ Serves 10–12

70% dark chocolate 300g, chopped
unsalted butter 150g
eggs 6, separated
golden caster sugar 40g
ground cardamom 1¼ tsp
cocoa powder, for dusting
CHOCOLATE SAUCE
milk chocolate 200g, chopped
ground cardamom 1 tsp

■ Heat the oven to 180C/fan 160C/gas 4. Line an 18cm springform cake tin with baking paper.

■ Melt the dark chocolate together with the butter in a heatproof bowl over a pan of simmering water or in the microwave. Beat the egg yolks, half the sugar and the cardamom until pale, very thick and creamy. Add the melted chocolate and mix well.

■ Whisk the egg whites and remaining sugar until stiff. Now carefully fold the egg whites into the chocolate mixture, making sure you stir it very gently. When mixed, spoon it all into the prepared tin and bake for 20–25 minutes. Set aside to cool. The finished torte should have a baked-mousse-like consistency.

■ For the chocolate sauce, bring 100ml water to the boil, add the milk chocolate and cardamom and whisk until thick and glossy. Dust the torte with cocoa powder and serve with the sauce.

Very lemony cake

1 hour 10 minutes ■ Serves 10

unsalted butter 250g, softened
golden caster sugar 250g
eggs 6 medium, lightly beaten
self-raising flour 300g
baking powder ½ tsp
cornflour 3 tbsp
unwaxed lemons 3, all zested, 2 juiced
lemon curd 300g jar
blueberries 150g
icing sugar to dust
ICING
caster sugar 175g
eggs 3 whites
unsalted butter 250g, diced and softened

■ Heat the oven to 180C/fan 160C/gas 4. Butter and base-line three 20cm cake tins. Beat the butter and sugar until pale and fluffy. Gradually add the eggs, beating well as you go. Sift the flour, baking powder and cornflour into the cake mixture and mix to make a smooth batter. Add two-thirds of the lemon zest and all the juice, then divide the mixture evenly between the tins, levelling the top. Bake for 30–35 minutes or until golden and cooked (test with a skewer). Cool in the tins for 5 minutes before turning out onto a wire rack.

■ For the icing, bring the caster sugar and 100ml water to the boil and cook until the syrup reaches 'soft ball' stage (it will form a squidgy ball when dropped into a glass of cold water). Whisk the egg whites until stiff. Still whisking, add the hot sugar syrup in a steady stream, then whisk for 3 minutes until the meringue begins to cool. Add the butter a little at a time, beating constantly. If the mixture curdles, don't panic, continue beating until it's smooth again.

■ Put a cake layer on a serving dish and spread with half the lemon curd. Top with another cake layer and the remaining lemon curd, then the final cake layer. Using a palette knife, spread the icing over the top and sides of the cake. Scatter over the blueberries and remaining lemon zest. Dust with icing sugar.

Ginger cake with fudge frosting

1 hour 30 minutes ■ Serves 18

CAKE

butter 225g

dark muscovado sugar 225g

golden syrup 225g

ground ginger 2 tsp

eggs 2

milk 300ml

plain flour 375g

bicarbonate of soda 2 tsp

FROSTING

butter 75g

double cream 175ml

sugar 175g

You can eat this cake straightaway, but it tastes even better if you leave it for 3 days to improve. When the cake is cold, wrap it in foil and store in a cool place.

■ Heat the oven to 150C/fan 130C/gas 2. Line a 24cm square cake tin with baking paper. Melt the butter, sugar and syrup in a pan set over a medium heat. Remove from the heat and leave to cool slightly. Then stir in the ground ginger, eggs and milk.

■ Sift the flour and bicarbonate of soda into a large bowl. Make a well in the centre, add the ginger mixture and blend together until smooth, using a large spoon or whisk. Pour the mixture into the cake tin and bake for 1 hour, until firm to the touch and a skewer inserted into the centre comes out clean. Remove from the oven and allow to cool completely.

■ Heat the frosting ingredients in a heavy-based pan over a moderate heat until melted. Bring to the boil and simmer for 5 minutes, stirring constantly and taking care that the frosting does not burn. Remove from the heat and whisk until just thickened to a pouring consistency. Leave to cool and set a little. Spread over the top of the cooled cake.

Baked raspberry cheesecake

1 hour ■ Serves 8

digestive biscuits 8

butter 50g, melted

cream cheese 600g

plain flour 2 tbsp

caster sugar 175g

vanilla extract

eggs 2, plus 1 yolk

soured cream 142ml carton

raspberries 250g

■ Heat the oven to 180C/fan 160C/gas 4. Crush the biscuits in a food processor (or put in a plastic bag and bash with a rolling pin). Mix with the butter. Press into a 20cm springform tin and bake for 5 minutes, then cool.

■ Beat the cream cheese with the flour, sugar, a few drops of vanilla, whole eggs, the yolk and soured cream until light and fluffy. Put a handful of whole raspberries into the base then pour over the cheese mixture.

■ Mash and sieve the rest of the raspberries and drizzle 2 tbsp of the purée over the top, running a knife through any large blobs. Bake for 40 minutes and then check; it should be set but slightly wobbly in the centre. Leave in the tin to cool. Serve with the rest of the sauce and some extra raspberries on the side.

Choc-hazelnut meringue cake

55 minutes ■ Serves 6

toasted hazelnuts 150g, whole or chopped
egg whites 5
golden caster sugar 275g
white wine vinegar 1 tbsp
dark chocolate 100g
mascarpone 250g tub
double cream 142ml carton

■ Heat the oven to 190C/fan 170C/gas 5. Line 2 x 18–20cm springform tins with foil and oil the foil.

■ Whizz the nuts in a food processor until finely ground. Whisk the egg whites in a bowl until stiff peaks form. Whisk in most of the sugar, a spoonful at a time, to make a shiny, stiff meringue. Stir the rest of the sugar into the nuts, then fold into the meringue with the vinegar. Divide between the tins and level the tops. Bake for 45–50 minutes, then cool in the tins in the oven.

■ When the meringues are cold, peel off the foil. Put a meringue, top-side down, on a plate. Melt the chocolate, then leave to cool a little. Whisk the mascarpone and cream together until spoonable, then fold through the chocolate. Spread a layer over the base and then put another meringue layer on top.

Lemon drizzle cake

1 hour 45 minutes ■ Serves 8

unsalted butter 225g, softened
golden caster sugar 225g
lemons 3 zested and 2 juiced
eggs 4, lightly whisked
self-raising flour 200g
baking powder 1 tsp
ground almonds 50g
icing sugar

■ Heat the oven to 180C/fan 160C/gas 4. Butter and line the base of a 20cm round cake tin. Beat the butter and caster sugar in a large bowl using an electric hand whisk until pale and creamy. Add the lemon zest (reserving some for decoration) and mix well. Whisk the eggs gradually into the butter mixture, beating well between each addition – don't worry if it curdles.

■ Sift together the flour and baking powder and fold into the cake mixture using a large metal spoon or spatula. Add the ground almonds and three-quarters of the lemon juice and fold until thoroughly combined. Spoon into the prepared cake tin and bake for 1 hour 15 minutes or until a skewer inserted into the middle of the cake comes out without any raw mix on it. Put the cake tin on a wire rack to cool for 10 minutes.

■ Meanwhile, mix together the remaining lemon juice and zest and enough icing sugar to make a runny icing and then drizzle over the top of the cake. Cool in the tin for a further 30 minutes and then remove from the tin and cool completely before serving.

Old-fashioned coffee and walnut cake

45 minutes ■ Serves 8

unsalted butter 175g, softened
golden caster sugar 175g
eggs 3
instant espresso coffee granules 3 tbsp, mixed with enough boiling water to make a paste
self-raising flour 175g
baking powder 2 tsp
walnut pieces 50g, toasted
ICING
unsalted butter 150g, softened
icing sugar 350g
instant espresso coffee granules 2–3 tsp, dissolved in 1 tbsp boiling water
walnut halves to decorate
icing sugar or **cocoa** to dust

■ Heat the oven to 180C/fan 160C/gas 4. Base-line and butter two 20cm sandwich tins. Beat the butter and caster sugar with electric beaters until fluffy. Beat in the eggs one by one, then the coffee, fold in the flour and baking powder. Add a little milk if the mixture is too thick (it should fall off a spoon) and then fold in the walnuts. Spoon into the sandwich tins and bake for 20–25 minutes. Cool on a wire rack.

■ Beat the butter and icing sugar until creamy (electric beaters will give more volume). Beat in the coffee a little at a time to taste. Sandwich the cooled cakes together with half the icing and then use the other half to decorate the top along with the walnut halves and a dusting of icing sugar or cocoa.

Sherry-soaked raisin and almond cake

1 hour + soaking ■ Serves 6

raisins 200g

sherry 250ml

butter 250g

caster sugar 250g

eggs 4, beaten

ground almonds 200g

polenta 100g

self-raising flour 100g

icing sugar to dust

extra sherry-soaked raisins and **vanilla ice-cream**, to serve

■ Heat the oven to 180C/fan 160C/gas 4. Butter and line the base of a 23cm springform cake tin.

■ Soak the raisins in 100ml of the sherry for about 30 minutes until they plump up. Put the butter and sugar into the bowl of a mixer and beat until very pale and fluffy. Keep the motor running and slowly add the eggs. Scrape down the sides and add the ground almonds, followed by the polenta and the flour. Add the raisins and their soaking liquid and beat slowly and briefly until evenly incorporated. Spoon the mixture into the prepared tin. Bake for 45–50 minutes until the cake is firm but springy to the touch.

■ Remove the cake from the oven, prick the surface with a cocktail stick or fine skewer and spoon the remaining 150ml sherry evenly across the surface of the cake. Leave to cool.

■ Dust with icing sugar just before serving. Serve as it is or with extra sherry-soaked raisins and vanilla ice cream for dessert.

Chocolate and banana cake

1 hour 15 minutes ■ Makes 2 cakes

dark chocolate 100g

unsalted butter 150g, softened

golden caster sugar 175g

eggs 3, beaten

self-raising flour 175g

baking powder 1 level tsp

cocoa powder 25g

bananas 2, large, peeled and mashed

STREUSEL TOPPING

unsalted butter 25g

plain flour 2 generous tbsp

demerara sugar 1 level tbsp

pecans chopped to make 2 tbsp

■ Heat the oven to 180C/fan 160C/gas 4. Butter and line the bases of two 450g loaf tins with baking parchment.

■ To make the streusel topping, rub the butter into the flour, then mix in the demerara sugar and chopped pecans.

■ Melt the chocolate either in the microwave or in a small heatproof bowl set over a pan of barely simmering water. Stir until smooth and remove from the heat.

■ Cream together the softened butter and caster sugar until pale and fluffy. Gradually add the eggs, beating well between each addition. Sift together the flour, baking powder and cocoa and fold in using a large metal spoon. Add the mashed banana and melted chocolate and mix well.

■ Divide the mixture between the 2 tins and top each with the streusel. Bake for about 45 minutes or until a skewer inserted in the middle comes out clean. Cool on a wire rack, then wrap in baking parchment or foil to keep.

Rosewater meringue cake

2 hours ■ Serves 8

egg whites 4 large

golden caster sugar 225g

cornflour 1/2 tbsp

white wine vinegar 1 tsp

rosewater

double cream 284ml carton

crystallised rose petals 3 tbsp

white chocolate 50g

■ Heat the oven to 150C/fan 130C/gas 2. Line two 20cm cake tins with foil, smoothing it down and folding the overhang over the edges of the tins.

■ Whisk the egg whites with an electric hand whisk until they form softly drooping peaks. Still whisking, add the sugar little by little, then whisk in the cornflour and vinegar. Add 1 tbsp rosewater and keep going until the mixture is thick and densely creamy.

■ Divide between the tins, leveling the surface. Cook for 1 1/2 hours and then leave to cool in the oven before carefully removing the foil. The meringues may crack as they cool – they won't look as perfect but will still taste divine.

■ A couple of hours before serving, whip the cream with 1 tsp rosewater until thick and stir in 2 tbsp rose petals. Use to sandwich the meringues together. Melt the chocolate in a microwave and drizzle over the top and sides of the cake. Finish with a scattering of the remaining rose petals.

Orange polenta cake

2 hours 30 minutes ■ Serves 8

oranges 2
eggs 5
golden caster sugar 250g
polenta 75g
ground almonds 175g
baking powder 1 tsp
ORANGE SYRUP
oranges 4
golden caster sugar 100g
cardamom pods 4
cinnamon stick 1

■ To make the cake, wash the oranges and put in a pan. Cover with water, bring to the boil, simmer, and cook for 1 hour. Remove from the heat and cool.

■ Heat the oven to 180C/fan 160C/gas 4. Butter, flour and line the base of a 23cm springform tin with baking parchment. Cut the oranges into quarters and remove any pips. Put the oranges in a food processor and pulse until well chopped but not completely puréed.

■ Whisk the eggs and caster sugar until thick and pale. Add the chopped oranges, polenta, ground almonds and baking powder. Pour into the tin and bake for about 1 hour or until a skewer pushed into the middle of the cake comes out clean. Cool the cake in the tin.

■ To make the orange syrup, peel the zest off 2 oranges using a vegetable peeler. Slice the zest into fine julienne strips and blanch for 1 minute in boiling water. Squeeze all the oranges and strain the juice.

■ Put the caster sugar into a small pan with 2 tbsp water over a low heat. Allow the sugar to melt and turn a deep amber-coloured caramel. Very carefully pour the orange juice into the pan (it will splutter) and bring to the boil. Add the blanched zest, cardamom and cinnamon and continue to cook until the caramel has melted and the syrup has thickened slightly. Serve warm with the cake.

Victoria sponge cake

1 hour ■ Serves 8

unsalted butter 225g, softened
golden caster sugar 225g
eggs 4, beaten
self-raising flour 225g, sifted
milk 2 tbsp
raspberry jam 3 tbsp
BUTTERCREAM
unsalted butter 125g, softened
icing sugar 3 tbsp, sifted, plus extra to dust
vanilla extract 1 tsp

■ Heat the oven to 180C/fan 160C/gas 4. Butter and line the bases of two 20cm sandwich tins with baking parchment.

■ To make the cake, cream the butter and sugar using an electric whisk until really pale and fluffy, this will take about 5 minutes. Gradually add the beaten eggs, 1 tbsp at a time, mixing well between each addition. Fold in the sifted flour and a small pinch of salt. Add the milk and mix until smooth.

■ Divide the batter between the tins. Bake for 25–30 minutes until pale golden and a skewer pushed in the middle of the cakes comes out clean. Cool in the tins for 5 minutes then turn out onto a wire rack and cool completely.

■ To make the buttercream, beat the butter, icing sugar and vanilla extract until pale and smooth then spread over the top of one of the cakes. Cover with a thick layer of raspberry jam and top with the other cake, pressing down gently. Dust with icing sugar before serving.

Chocolate tiramisu torte

1 hour ■ Serves 12

unsalted butter 300g, at room temperature
self-raising flour 270g
baking powder 1½ tsp
golden caster sugar 300g
eggs 6
cocoa powder 4 tbsp
instant coffee 2 tbsp, dissolved in 1 tbsp
boiling water
FILLING
espresso or **strong instant coffee** 100ml,
cooled
Tia Maria 4 tbsp
mascarpone 250ml tub
double cream 568ml carton
Amaretto 1 tbsp
dark chocolate 50g, finely grated

■ Heat the oven to 180C/fan 160C/gas 4.
Butter and line the base of two 20cm
cake tins.

■ Put all the cake ingredients into a
food processor and blend until smooth.
Divide between the tins and cook for
25–30 minutes or until the sponge is
springy. Cool completely then cut each
cake in half horizontally.

■ To make the filling, mix the coffee with
2 tbsp of the Tia Maria and sprinkle over
the cut sides of each cake. Beat the
mascarpone until it softens then stir in
the cream, bit by bit. Add the remaining
Tia Maria and the Amaretto then whisk
until softly whipped.

■ Sandwich the 4 layers together with the
boozy cream, leaving plenty for the top.
Finish the top with a layer of cream and
finely grated dark chocolate. Chill for an hour
before serving to make the cake easier to cut.

Fluffy coconut and lime cake

1 hour + cooling ■ Serves 10

caster sugar 200g

butter 200g, softened

eggs 4, beaten

self-raising flour 200g

baking powder 1 tsp

lime 1, zested and juiced

creamed coconut ½ x 200g block, grated

sweetened coconut flakes to decorate

FROSTING

eggs 2, whites only

granulated sugar 200g

vanilla extract ½ tsp

■ Heat the oven to 190C/fan 170C/gas 5. Line two 20cm sandwich tins. Beat the sugar, butter, eggs, flour, baking powder, lime zest and juice and creamed coconut together. Divide between the cake tins, level off the surface and bake for 20 minutes or until risen and golden. Cool completely.

■ To make the frosting, whisk the egg whites to stiff peaks. Combine the sugar with 4 tbsp water and boil until you have a thick, clear syrup. Beat the syrup into the egg whites, adding it in a thin stream, and stir in the vanilla. Sandwich the cakes together with frosting then frost the top and sides. Gently press flakes of coconut all over the sides.

Angel cake

1 hour ■ Serves 8

plain flour 125g, sifted
egg whites 6
cream of tartar ½ tsp or a squeeze of
lemon juice
golden caster sugar 175g
vanilla extract 1 tsp
orange 1, zest grated
lemon 1, zest grated
GLACE ICING
icing sugar 200g, sifted
orange or **lemon juice** 2 tbsp

■ Heat the oven to 180C/fan 160C/gas 4.
Butter and flour a 23cm kugelhopf
(deep ring) tin.

■ Whisk the egg whites with the cream
of tartar or lemon juice in a clean, dry
bowl until they just hold a stiff peak. Add
the sugar a little at a time, whisking well
between each addition. Fold the flour into
the mixture along with the vanilla extract
and orange and lemon zests. Spoon the
mixture into the tin, spread level and give
the tin a sharp tap on the work surface to
knock out any large air bubbles.

■ Bake for 20–25 minutes until the cake is
springy and a skewer pushed in the middle
comes out clean. Invert the tin over a wire
rack and allow the cake to cool upside down
in the tin. The cake will drop out of the tin
and onto the wire rack as it shrinks.

■ To make the icing, beat together the
icing sugar and orange or lemon juice
and mix until smooth. Drizzle over the top
of the cooled cake, allowing the icing to run
down the sides of the cake. Let the icing set
before serving.

Sticky gingerbread

1 hour 40 minutes ■ Serves 12

unsalted butter 125g, softened

golden syrup 150g

black treacle 225g

bicarbonate of soda 1 tsp

light muscovado sugar 125g

egg 1, beaten

stem ginger in syrup 4 pieces, finely chopped

ground ginger 2 rounded tsp

ground cinnamon 1 rounded tsp

ground cloves ½ tsp

self-raising flour 300g

■ Heat the oven to 180C/fan 160C/gas 4. Butter a 20cm square cake tin and line the base and sides with baking parchment.

■ Mix 350ml boiling water with the golden syrup, black treacle and bicarbonate of soda. Cool.

■ Cream the butter and sugar until light and fluffy using an electric whisk. Gradually mix in the egg then add the ginger. Sift together the spices, flour and a pinch of salt. Fold one-third of the dry ingredients into the butter mixture followed by one-third of the cooled syrup. Add alternately and mix until smooth.

■ Pour into the cake tin and bake for about 1 hour or until a skewer pushed into the middle of the cake comes out with no raw mixture. Cool completely in the tin and then wrap tightly in foil. Best made 24 hours before serving.

Rich chocolate cake

2 hours ■ Serves 10

unsalted butter 200g

70% dark chocolate 300g

eggs 6, separated

caster sugar 200g

ground almonds 150g

lemon a squeeze of juice

FROSTING

apricot jam 4 rounded tbsp

icing sugar

marzipan 500g pack

70% dark chocolate 200g

unsalted butter 75g

double cream 2 tbsp

■ Heat the oven to 180C/fan 160C/gas 4. Butter, flour and base-line a 23cm springform tin.

■ Melt the chocolate and butter together either in a microwave or in a bowl over a pan of simmering water. Stir until smooth. Whisk the egg yolks with the sugar using an electric whisk until pale and very thick. Mix in the melted chocolate and butter. Stir in the ground almonds.

■ In a clean, dry bowl, whisk the egg whites and lemon juice together until just stiff peaks. Stir a large spoonful of the egg whites into the chocolate to loosen the mixture and then fold in the rest. Spoon into the tin and bake for about 1 hour until a crust forms and a skewer pushed into the middle of the cake comes out with cooked-looking crumbs. Cool in the tin completely.

■ Put the cake on a wire rack. If the cake is uneven, slice the top crust off to make a completely flat surface. Melt the jam, sieve and use to brush the top and sides of the cake. Dust your work surface with a little icing sugar and roll the marzipan out in a large, thin circle. Lay over the cake, covering the top and sides. Trim off any excess. Brush with a little more jam.

■ Melt the chocolate, butter and double cream together. Stir until smooth. Cool slightly. Pour almost all of the icing over the top of the cake and use a palette knife to smooth the rest over the sides. Leave in a cool place to allow the icing to set.

Ginger cheesecake

1 hour 20 minutes ■ Serves 8

ginger biscuits 10
butter 25g, melted
cream cheese 600g
plain flour 1 tbsp
eggs 2
vanilla extract 1 tsp
golden caster sugar 100g
soured cream 284ml carton
crystallised ginger 100g, chopped
icing sugar for dusting (optional)

■ Heat the oven to 180C/fan 160C/gas 4. Crush the biscuits in a food processor (or put in a plastic bag, seal and bash with a rolling pin). Add the melted butter and mix well. Press the crumbs into the base of a buttered 20cm springform tin and bake for 5 minutes. Cool.

■ Beat the cream cheese with the flour, eggs, vanilla, sugar and half of the soured cream until smooth. Stir in the crystallised ginger and pour the lot into the tin – the mix will be quite runny so the ginger will sink to the bottom.

■ Bake for 40 minutes and then check to see if the cheesecake is set but still slightly wobbly in the centre. Give it another 10 minutes if it isn't. Spoon over the remaining soured cream and bake for 5 minutes. Cool in the tin. Dust with icing sugar, if you like.

Chocolate and raspberry torte

1 hour 15 minutes ■ Serves 8

unsalted butter 50g

dark chocolate 200g, broken into pieces

eggs 4, separated

golden caster sugar 200g

cocoa powder 2 tbsp

self-raising flour 2 tbsp

raspberries 200g

icing sugar to serve

■ Heat the oven to 180C/fan 160C/gas 4. Line a 23cm square cake tin or brownie tin with parchment and butter it.

■ Melt the chocolate with the butter in a microwave or in a heatproof bowl set over barely simmering water.

■ Whisk the egg yolks and 100g sugar until light and fluffy. Stir in the cocoa powder and flour then fold in the chocolate mixture. In a clean dry bowl, beat the egg whites until stiff, then beat in the rest of the sugar.

■ Fold the egg whites into the chocolate (if the mixture is stiff, do this a little at a time until it loosens). Bake for 40 minutes or until a skewer comes out clean. Cool, then cut into squares and arrange the raspberries on top. Dust with icing sugar, to serve.

Orange and chocolate cake

40 minutes + cooling ■ Serves 8

orange 1, whole
caster sugar 125g
dark chocolate 200g, melted
ground almonds 100g
eggs 3, separated
baking powder ½ tsp
icing sugar, for dusting

■ Put the orange in a microwave-proof bowl. Add 250ml water, cover with clingfilm and microwave on High for 20 minutes, turning halfway through (or simmer for 1 hour in a small pan). Leave to cool, still covered.

■ Heat the oven to 180C/fan 160C/gas 4. Line a 20cm round springform tin with baking parchment. Cut the orange in half and remove the pips. Put in the food processor with 5 tbsp of the orangey liquid left in the bowl and blitz to a smooth purée, scraping down the bowl a couple of times. Add the sugar, melted chocolate, almonds, egg yolks and baking powder, and whizz again to mix thoroughly. Tip into a large bowl.

■ Beat the egg whites until stiff, but not dry, and fold into the chocolate mixture. Spoon into the lined tin. Put the tin on a baking sheet, then in the oven. Bake for 1 hour, covering with a piece of foil or baking parchment halfway through to stop the top burning. Cool in the tin. Dust with icing sugar before serving, if you like.

Carrot cake

2 hours + cooling ■ Serves 12

plain flour 300g

cinnamon 2 tsp

baking powder 1 tsp

bicarbonate of soda ½ tsp

soft brown sugar 200g

eggs 4

oil 250ml

orange 1, zested

lemon 1, zested

carrots 200g, finely grated

walnuts 150g, chopped

pineapple pieces 227g tin, well drained
and chopped (optional)

CREAM CHEESE FROSTING

unsalted butter 125g, at room temperature

icing sugar 50g

cream cheese 250g

■ Heat the oven to 150C/fan 130C/gas 2. Line a 20 x 10cm deep cake tin. Sift the flour, cinnamon, baking powder and bicarbonate of soda together and stir in the sugar. Beat the eggs with the oil and citrus zests. Stir in the carrots and fold everything into the flour mixture. Fold in the walnuts and pineapple, if using. Spoon the mixture into the tin and bake for 1 hour 20 minutes or until a skewer comes out clean. Cool.

■ For the frosting, beat the butter and icing sugar together until soft and then beat in the cream cheese. Chill the mixture until it's thick but spreadable. Spread a thick layer on top of the cake, making sure the side of the icing is flat and continues upwards from the side of the cake.

Posh yule log

1 hour ■ Serves 10

cocoa powder 50g, plus extra for dusting
self-raising flour 75g
baking powder 1 tsp
eggs 5 large
caster sugar 100g, plus extra for dusting
FILLING
double cream 284ml carton
Baileys 6 tbsp
TOPPING
butter 300g
icing sugar 100g, plus extra for
dusting
dark chocolate 400g, melted

■ Heat the oven to 190C/fan 170C/gas 5. Line a 30 x 40cm Swiss roll tin with baking parchment, butter and dust with cocoa. Sift the flour, baking powder and cocoa into a bowl. Beat the eggs and caster sugar with an electric mixer until thick, pale and trebled in volume, about 8 minutes.

■ Fold in the flour mix with a large metal spoon – the less air you squash the better, so do this carefully but quickly. Pour into the tin, tipping the tin as you pour so the batter is even. Bake for 10–15 minutes or until firm to the touch.

■ Cool the sponge for 2 minutes then turn it out onto a piece of baking parchment dusted with caster sugar. Peel off the lining paper and roll the sponge up using the paper underneath. It may crack a bit but don't worry. Leave to cool.

■ For the filling, whisk the double cream until it is stiff and stir in the Baileys.

■ For the topping, beat the butter and icing sugar together and fold in the melted chocolate. Leave until cool enough to spread.

■ Gently unroll the sponge and dot blobs of the topping over with a teaspoon, use just under half the mixture. Spread out gently. Spread over the Baileys cream and reroll the roulade as tightly as you can, using the paper to help you, without squashing out the filling.

■ Spread the remaining topping over the roulade, using a palette knife to give a rough surface, and dust with cocoa or icing sugar.

Mango upside-down cake

1 hour 20 minutes ■ Serves 8

unsalted butter 40g
golden caster sugar 275g
mangoes 4 small, or 2 large
unsalted butter 175g, softened
eggs 3, beaten
plain flour 225g
baking powder 2 tsp
milk 75ml, at room temperature

■ Heat the oven to 180C/fan 160C/gas 4. Butter a solid-based 22cm round cake tin.
■ Put 100g caster sugar and 2 tbsp water in a small pan over a low heat to allow the sugar to dissolve. Bring to the boil and continue to cook without stirring until the sugar has turned a deep caramel colour.

Add 40g butter and swirl the pan to incorporate evenly. Pour immediately into the cake tin, covering the base with an even layer of caramel. Leave to cool.
■ Peel the mangoes, cut off the cheeks and slice into wedges. Slice the rest of the mango flesh and arrange all over the hard caramel in the cake tin.
■ Cream the softened butter and the remaining caster sugar until pale and fluffy. Gradually add the beaten eggs, mixing well between each addition. Sift the flour, baking powder and a pinch of salt together and fold into the cake mixture using a large metal spoon. Add the milk and mix until smooth.
■ Carefully spoon the cake mixture over the mango slices and level. Bake for about 45–50 minutes or until a skewer inserted into the middle of the cake comes out clean. Allow the cake to cool in the tin for 5 minutes before turning out onto a serving dish.

Lemon curd and raspberry roulade

1 hour ■ Serves 10

butter 25g melted, for brushing
caster sugar 180g, plus some for dusting
plain flour 100g
baking powder 1 tsp
eggs 6, separated
lemon 1, zested and juiced (you need
2 tbsp juice)
whipping cream 284ml carton
lemon curd 1 jar
raspberries 250g
icing sugar for dusting

■ Heat the oven to 180C/fan 160C/gas 4.
Line a 34 x 24cm Swiss roll tin or baking tray
with baking parchment, leaving about 1cm
over the sides of the tin. Brush with butter
and dust with caster sugar.

■ Sift the flour and baking powder together.
Beat the egg yolks, lemon zest and juice and
sugar together with electric beaters until
very light and thick. Sift in the flour and fold
in. Whisk the egg whites until firm and then
fold into the cake mix without squashing out
too much air.

■ Spoon into the tin, level the top and bake
for 15–20 minutes until golden brown and a
skewer comes out clean. Cool for 10 minutes
and then turn out onto another piece of
baking parchment dusted with caster sugar.
While the cake is still warm, roll it up so it
looks like a Swiss roll. Cool.

■ Unroll the roulade as much as you can – it
can be tricky to unroll the very last bit. Whip
the cream until thick and fold it together with
the lemon curd. Spread this over the roulade
without getting too close to the edges, it will
squash out as it rolls. Dot all over with
raspberries. Roll up and dust with icing sugar.

Orange blossom and yoghurt cake

1 hour ■ Serves 8

self-raising flour 200g, sifted
ground almonds 100g
caster sugar 150g
baking powder 1 tsp
eggs 2 large, beaten with a fork
Greek yoghurt 250g
sunflower oil 150ml
lemon 1, zested
ORANGE SYRUP
water 150ml
caster sugar 175g
orange 1, juiced and 2 strips of zest
lemon ½, juiced
cardamom pods 5, crushed
orange flower water 1 tbsp (look in the baking section of larger supermarkets or buy from Middle Eastern shops)
icing sugar and **crème fraîche** or **Greek yoghurt** to serve

■ To make the syrup, put the water, sugar, zest, citrus juices and cardamom into a pan. Heat gently, stirring to help the sugar dissolve. Bring to the boil and simmer for 7 minutes. It will thicken and become syrupy as it cools. Cool, then strain and add the orange flower water.

■ Heat the oven to 180C/fan 160C/gas 4. Butter or oil a 20cm springform tin. Put all the dry ingredients for the cake in a bowl with a good pinch of salt and make a well in the centre. Put all the rest of the ingredients in the well and stir with a wooden spoon, gradually incorporating the wet ingredients. Spoon into the tin and bake for half an hour. A skewer pushed into the middle of the cake should come out clean, if not, give it a little longer.

■ Leave for 10 minutes to cool in the tin, then turn out onto a plate. Pierce all over with a skewer and, while the cake is still warm, slowly pour over the syrup. Leave to soak in.

■ Dust with icing sugar just before serving – the sugar just disappears into the syrupy top otherwise – and serve with crème fraîche or yoghurt.

Tiramisu cake

1 hour 15 minutes ■ Serves 12

butter 300g
caster sugar 300g
eggs 4
self-raising flour 300g
FILLING
caster sugar 4 tsp
espresso coffee 2 shots (or make up 60ml of very strong coffee)
mascarpone 250g tub
icing sugar to taste
TOPPING
dark chocolate 200g
butter 50g

■ Heat the oven to 180C/fan 160C/gas 4. Line 2 square 20 x 20cm cake tins with parchment and butter.

■ Cream the butter and sugar together until smooth and pale, gradually beat in the eggs and then fold in the flour. If the mixture is very heavy, add 1–2 tbsp water. Spoon into the cake tins and bake for 20–30 minutes or until risen and golden and a skewer inserted into the middle comes out clean. Cool.

■ Peel the paper off the cakes and trim the top flat on each. Line 1 tin with a double layer of clingfilm. Add the sugar to the espresso and stir until dissolved. Drop a cake back in the tin, trimmed-side up, and brush over half of the espresso. Brush the remaining espresso over the trimmed side of the other cake.

■ Whip the mascarpone (with electric beaters) until it is spoonable then add enough icing sugar to sweeten it, around 3 tbsp. Spoon over the cake and then carefully drop the other cake on top, espresso-side down. Press down firmly.

■ Melt the chocolate and butter together in a microwave or in a heatproof bowl set over barely simmering water. Let it cool and thicken slightly then pour in an even layer onto the cake. Leave to set somewhere cool. Lift out the cake using the clingfilm and carefully peel it off.

Lemon polenta cake with Limoncello syrup

1 hour 15 minutes ■ Serves 8

butter 250g, softened
caster sugar 250g
eggs 3
polenta 100g
ground almonds 250g
baking powder 1 tsp
lemons 3, all zested, 1 juiced
limoncello 4 tbsp
icing sugar 3 tbsp

■ Heat the oven to 160C/fan 140C/gas 3. Butter and base-line a 23cm springform tin. Beat together the butter and sugar until light and fluffy.

■ Add the eggs one by one, beating between each addition. Fold in the polenta, almonds and baking powder, then stir in the lemon zest and juice.

■ Bake for about 50 minutes – 1 hour until the cake is risen and golden (cover the top of the cake loosely with foil after 30 minutes to stop it browning too much). Meanwhile, put the limoncello and icing sugar in a small pan and warm gently to make a syrup. Serve the cake warm with a drizzle of limoncello syrup.

Caramel orange and poppy seed cake

1 hour 30 minutes + cooling ■ Serves 10

oranges 2, zested and juiced
poppy seeds 30g
milk 100ml
butter 200g, at room temperature
caster sugar 175g
eggs 3
self-raising flour 300g
baking powder ½ tsp
CARAMELISED ORANGES
caster sugar 125g
oranges 2, sliced
ICING
caster sugar 100g

■ To make the caramelised oranges, put the caster sugar in a frying pan in an even layer and heat until it starts to melt and turn a golden colour. Tip the pan from side to side to keep the caramel as even as you can. Once it reaches a dark gold, carefully add half the orange juice from the cake oranges (it will splutter so stand back). Keep on the heat, stirring so that any lumps melt back into the caramel. Add the orange slices and heat gently for about 5 minutes until they soften a little. Lift out and drain, keep the caramel and orange slices for later.

■ Heat the oven to 160C/fan 140C/gas 3. Stir the poppy seeds and milk in a bowl. Beat the butter, orange zest and sugar with an electric mixer until light and creamy. Gradually beat in the eggs. Sift in the flour and baking powder and add the poppy seeds and milk. Stir, then spoon half into a 900g loaf tin lined with baking parchment. Add a layer of caramelised orange slices and cover with the rest of the mixture. Bake for 55–60 minutes or until cooked when tested with a skewer.

■ To make the icing, add the sugar to the remaining orange juice and stir. Add to the caramel but don't try to dissolve the sugar. Pour over the hot cake while it is in the tin, lay the rest of the orange slices down the centre and leave to cool. Remove from the tin when cold.

Strawberry and passion fruit meringue roulade

50 minutes ■ Serves 8

egg whites 4

caster sugar 200g

lemon curd 200g

passion fruit 3, strain the seeds and keep both the seeds and the juice

double cream 150ml

strawberries 10, hulled and chopped

icing sugar, for dusting

■ Heat the oven to 180C/fan 160C/gas 4. Line a 23 x 30cm Swiss roll tin with baking paper. Whisk the egg whites with a pinch of salt until stiff. Slowly add the sugar, still whisking, until stiff and glossy. Spoon the mixture evenly into the tin and bake for 15 minutes, until crisp on the outside. Remove and cool completely.

■ Lay a piece of fresh baking paper out and flip the meringue over onto it, carefully pull away the used paper and discard. Spread the lemon curd over the meringue and then the passion fruit seeds.

■ Whip the cream with the passion fruit juice and spread on top of the lemon curd. Sprinkle over the strawberries. Roll the meringue up lengthways. Dust with icing sugar to serve.

Sticky toffee cheesecake

1 hour 40 minutes + cooling ■ Serves 8

shortbread fingers or **biscuits** 8

butter 50g, melted

cream cheese or **curd cheese** 600g

golden caster sugar 100g

plain flour 3 tbsp

vanilla extract 2 tsp

eggs 3

soured cream 142ml carton

white chocolate 300g, melted

hard caramels 6, roughly chopped

caramel or **dulche de leche** 225g jar

■ Heat the oven to 180C/fan 160C/gas 4. Crush the biscuits in a food processor, stir in the butter and press the mixture into the base of a 20cm springform tin. Bake for 10 minutes, then cool. Turn the oven down to 140C/fan 120C/gas 1.

■ Beat the cream cheese with the sugar, flour and vanilla. Add the eggs, soured cream and chocolate and combine. Sprinkle the hard caramels over the biscuit base, pour the cheesecake mixture carefully on top and bake for 40–50 minutes, the filling should still have a slight wobble when it is cooked. Cool, then spread a layer of caramel or dulche de leche on top. Chill until needed.

Lemon and vanilla cheesecake with candied lemon peel

1 hour 10 minutes ■ Serves 8–10

ready-made flan sponge 1 large
golden caster sugar 225g
cornflour 3 tbsp
low-fat cream cheese 750g
eggs 2, lightly beaten
lemons 3, zested
vanilla pod 1, seeds scraped out
half-fat crème fraîche 300ml
CANDIED LEMON PEEL
lemon 1
caster sugar 100g

■ To make the candied peel, cut long strips of peel from the lemon then cut into thin julienne strips. Put in a pan and cover with 100ml cold water. Add the sugar and gently bring to the boil, stirring, until the sugar has dissolved. Simmer for 30 minutes. Leave to cool. While cooling, heat the oven to 180C/fan 160C /gas 4.

■ Lightly butter a 25cm springform cake tin. Trim the sponge so it neatly sits in the flat base of the tin. Mix the sugar and cornflour in a large bowl. Add the cream cheese and beat well until it has blended to a creamy texture. Beat in the eggs, lemon zest, vanilla and crème fraîche, until smooth. Pour on top of the sponge base.

■ Wrap the bottom third of the tin in clingfilm or foil to prevent any leaks and sit in a roasting tray. Pour in enough hot water to just cover the base of the tray. Put in the oven and bake for 50–55 minutes until the cheesecake is just set and golden on top. Top up the water halfway through if needed.

■ Remove the cheesecake from the oven and either cool at room temperature for a soft creamy texture, or chill for a few hours or overnight for a firm dense texture. Spoon over the candied lemon peel before serving.

Ginger, cherry and macadamia nut cookies

45 minutes ■ Makes 24

butter 50g, softened

golden granulated sugar 60g

light muscovado sugar 60g

egg 1

vanilla extract ½ tsp

self-raising flour 150g

semi-dried cherries 70g

macadamia nuts 50g, chopped

stem ginger in syrup 2 pieces from a jar, chopped

root ginger walnut-sized piece, grated

icing sugar for dusting

■ Heat the oven to 180C/fan 160C/gas 4. Line 2 baking sheets with baking parchment. Beat together the butter, sugars, egg and vanilla. Stir in the flour, then the cherries, nuts and both gingers. Drop heaped teaspoons of the mixture 5cm apart on the baking sheets.

■ Bake for 12–14 minutes until lightly browned. Leave on the baking sheet for 5 minutes before lifting onto a wire rack to cool. Dust with icing sugar. The cookies keep in a tin for up to a week.

Soft-baked white chocolate and macadamia cookies

45 minutes ■ Makes 30 large cookies

unsalted butter 225g, softened
light muscovado sugar 200g
vanilla extract 1 tsp
eggs 2, beaten
plain flour 300g
bicarbonate of soda 1 tsp
desiccated coconut 75g
white chocolate 250g, chopped
macadamia nuts 150g, chopped

■ Heat the oven to 180C/fan 160C/gas 4. Line 2 solid baking sheets with baking parchment.

■ Cream the butter and sugar with an electric whisk until light and fluffy. Mix the vanilla and eggs and add to the butter and sugar. Sift the flour, bicarbonate of soda and a pinch of salt into the butter mix and fold in. Add the coconut, chocolate and nuts and mix in.

■ Drop rounded tablespoons of the mixture onto the baking sheets, leaving about 4cm between each cookie. Bake for about 10–15 minutes until golden brown (you might need to do this in batches). Cool on the baking sheets and then store in an airtight box.

Cashew tuiles

1 hour ■ Makes 40

unsalted butter 80g
caster sugar 100g
golden syrup 3 tbsp
double cream 1 tbsp
plain flour 75g
salt ½ tsp
roasted salted cashews 75g, chopped

■ Heat the oven to 180C/fan 160C/gas 4. Line a baking sheet with non-stick baking paper. In a pan, combine the butter, sugar, golden syrup and cream. Bring to the boil over a medium heat, stirring constantly. Add the flour and salt and cook until the batter is slightly thickened, about 1 minute.

■ Stir in the nuts. Drop teaspoons of batter 10cm apart on the baking sheet. Bake until golden, about 6 minutes. Cool on the baking sheet for about 3 minutes. It's important that these don't get too cold or they'll set. If they do set, put them back in the oven for 30 seconds to soften them.

■ Quickly and carefully, use a spatula to lift the tuile off the sheet and put it on a rolling pin. It should shape itself but may need a little help – just ease it round the rolling pin with a spatula. Leave to set for a minute then put on a wire rack. Repeat until the dough is finished.

Jammy biscuits

45 minutes + chilling ■ Makes 20

unsalted butter 225g, softened
caster sugar 150g
vanilla extract 1 tsp
egg yolks 3, beaten
plain flour 250g
ground almonds 110g
raspberry and **apricot jam** for spreading
icing sugar to dust

■ Beat the butter and caster sugar together until pale and fluffy. Add the vanilla and egg yolks and mix thoroughly. Gradually add the flour and ground almonds. Lightly knead the mixture until it comes together in a ball. Wrap and chill for 1 hour.

■ Heat the oven to 170C/fan 150C/gas 5. Roll the dough out to the thickness of a £1 coin on a lightly floured surface and stamp out biscuits using a 6–7cm cutter. Reshape the leftover dough into a ball, re-roll and cut out more biscuits. Stamp out a smaller circle from the middles of half the biscuits.

■ Put the biscuits on lined baking sheets and bake for 12–15 minutes or until golden. You may need to do these in batches. Rest for a minute then transfer to a wire rack. When completely cold, spread the whole biscuits with either jam. Dust the ring-shaped biscuits with icing sugar. Put a sugar-dusted ring on top of a jam-covered biscuit and press lightly together.

Allspice chocolate florentines

20 minutes + cooling ■ Makes 25

butter 75g

golden caster sugar 5 tbsp

plain flour 3 tbsp

almonds, pecans or **hazelnuts** 50g, chopped

chopped mixed peel 50g

sultanas 25g, chopped

glacé cherries 25g, chopped

milk chocolate 150g, chopped

allspice 1/4 tsp

dried chillies, freshly ground, a good pinch

■ Heat the oven to 180C/fan 160C/gas 4. Line a large baking sheet with baking paper. Heat the butter and sugar together in a pan until the sugar dissolves. Mix in the flour then add the nuts, mixed peel, sultanas and cherries.

■ Put teaspoonfuls of the mixture quite widely spaced onto the baking sheet and flatten slightly. You may have to make 2 batches. Bake for 10 minutes. While still hottish, neaten up the edges using the side of a knife. Let them cool.

■ Melt the chocolate in a heatproof bowl over a pan of simmering water or in the microwave. Add the allspice and chillies and mix well. Spread over the flat side of the florentines and cool before serving.

Double chocolate brownies

1 hour ■ Makes 18

unsalted butter 175g, plus extra for greasing
dark chocolate 250g
golden caster sugar 250g
eggs 3
vanilla extract 1 tsp
plain flour 150g
walnuts or **pecans** 150g, toasted and roughly chopped
milk chocolate chips 200g, or roughly chopped chocolate

■ Heat the oven to 180C/fan 160C/gas 4. Butter and line the base and sides of a 30 x 20 x 3cm baking tin with baking parchment.

■ Melt the butter and dark chocolate together either in a heatproof bowl set over a pan of simmering water, or in the microwave on a low setting. Stir until smooth and then leave to cool a little.

■ Whisk the sugar and eggs together with an electric whisk until pale and thick. Mix in the vanilla, melted butter and chocolate. Sift the flour and fold into the batter with the chopped nuts and chocolate chips. Pour the batter into the tin and bake for 35 minutes. Cool in the tin then cut into squares.

Star cookies

1 hour ■ Makes 40

egg white 1
sugar crystals or **silver balls** to decorate
SUGAR COOKIE DOUGH
unsalted butter 200g, at room
temperature
caster sugar 150g
vanilla extract 2 tsp
egg 1
plain flour 300g, sifted, plus extra
for dusting

■ Cream the butter and sugar in the bowl of an electric mixer, or use a large bowl with a hand-held electric beater. Beat in the vanilla and egg, then add the flour. Beat until smooth, remove from the bowl, halve, and shape into discs. Wrap with clingfilm and chill for about 40 minutes until firm.

■ Heat the oven to 180/fan 160C/gas 4. Dust the worksurface with flour and roll out 1 portion of dough to 3mm thick. Cut stars or other shapes with cutters. Line 2 baking sheets with non-stick baking paper and lift the cookies onto it using a palette knife.

■ Chill for 10 minutes and then bake for 10–12 minutes until just turning golden at the edges. Cool on a wire rack. When cool, brush lightly with egg white then sprinkle with sugar crystals and silver balls.

Iced and spiced biscuits

30 minutes + chilling/setting ■ Makes 40

plain flour 300g, plus extra for dusting
baking powder ½ tsp
mixed spice 1 tsp
ground cinnamon ½ tsp
unsalted butter 100g, softened
golden caster sugar 200g
egg 1 large, beaten
royal icing sugar 250g pack
food colourings

■ Sift the flour, baking powder, spices and a pinch of salt together. Cream together the butter and sugar until pale and fluffy, then gradually beat in the egg. Add the dry ingredients and mix thoroughly. Add a tsp of cold water to bring the dough together, if you need to. Press into a disc, wrap and chill for at least 30 minutes.

■ Heat the oven to 180C/fan 160C/gas 4. On a lightly floured surface, roll out the dough to the thickness of a £1 coin and, using cookie cutters, stamp out shapes. Lift onto parchment-lined baking sheets and bake for 15–20 minutes, or until pale golden in colour.

■ When the biscuits have cooled completely, mix up the royal icing with a little water, a bit at a time, until it is a spreadable consistency. Divide the icing into batches, then add the colours you want. Dip one side of each biscuit into one colour, then pipe on strips of other colours. Drag the point of a knife across the biscuits at right angles to the lines to make a pattern. Allow to set.

Marbled brownies

1 hour 30 minutes ■ Makes 18

unsalted butter 200g
dark chocolate 200g
caster sugar 250g
eggs 3
plain flour 125g
CREAM CHEESE MIX
cream cheese 400g
vanilla extract 1 tsp
caster sugar 125g
eggs 2

■ Heat the oven to 180C/fan 160C/gas 4. Butter and line a 20 x 30cm deep baking tin with baking parchment.

■ To make the cream cheese mix, beat together the cream cheese, vanilla extract, caster sugar and eggs until smooth and creamy.

■ To make the brownie mix, melt the chocolate and butter in a heatproof bowl set over a pan of barely simmering water, or in 20-second blasts in the microwave. Stir until smooth then cool slightly.

■ In another bowl, whisk together the caster sugar and eggs. Add the melted chocolate and butter mix and stir until combined. Sift the flour and fold into the mixture. Pour three-quarters of the chocolate mix into the prepared tin and level with a palette knife. Spoon over the cream cheese mix. Add the remaining chocolate mixture in dollops and tap the tin sharply on the work surface to level the mixtures. Using a skewer, marble the mixtures together.

■ Bake for 35–45 minutes, until just set in the middle. Cool in the tin before cutting into squares.

Chocolate crinkle cookies

40 minutes + chilling ■ Makes 20

dark chocolate 175g, chopped
unsalted butter 4 tbsp
plain flour 175g
baking powder ½ tsp
eggs 2, at room temperature
caster sugar 150g
vanilla extract 1 tsp
icing sugar 60g

■ Heat the oven to 160C/fan 140C/gas 3. Melt the chocolate and butter in a heatproof bowl over a small pan of simmering water, or in a microwave, until smooth. Cool slightly. In a separate bowl, mix the flour, baking powder and ½ tsp salt.

■ Beat the eggs and sugar with an electric whisk until pale, about 2 minutes. Reduce the speed and add the chocolate mix and vanilla extract. Add the flour mixture until blended together. Cover the bowl and chill for 1½ hours or even up to 2 days.

■ Put the icing sugar in a small bowl. Shape the dough into 4cm balls and roll in the sugar. Put them on baking sheets lined with baking paper and press down lightly with your hand to flatten. Bake for 12–15 minutes for soft centres and set edges. Let cool on the baking sheets for 5 minutes and then put on a wire rack to cool completely.

Lemon melting moments

45 minutes ■ Makes 12

unsalted butter 175g, softened

icing sugar 40g, sifted

lemons 2, zest grated

plain flour 150g, sifted

cornflour 40g, sifted

mascarpone 2 rounded tbsp

lemon curd 2 rounded tsp

■ Heat the oven to 180C/fan 160C/gas 4. Line a baking sheet with baking parchment. Cream the butter and icing sugar with an electric whisk until smooth and pale. Add the grated zest from 1½ lemons. Add the plain flour and cornflour and mix well – the mixture will become quite soft.

■ Divide into 24 even-sized balls and space well apart on the baking sheet (you could also pipe the mixture out for a more decorative finish, as pictured). Flatten each biscuit a little with your fingertips. Dip a fork into cold water and then press it gently into each biscuit. Bake for about 12–14 minutes until pale golden. Cool on the baking sheet.

■ Mix the remaining lemon zest, mascarpone and lemon curd. Sandwich the melting moments together with the lemony mascarpone. Don't keep them for longer than a couple of hours or they'll go soggy.

Raspberry and chocolate brownie cakes

30 minutes ■ Makes 8

70% dark chocolate 100g

butter 100g

eggs 2, beaten

golden caster sugar 230g

self-raising flour 100g

raspberries 150g

icing sugar for dusting

■ Heat the oven to 180C/fan 160C/gas 4. Melt the chocolate and butter in a pan over a low heat and mix together. Remove from the heat and beat in the eggs, sugar and flour. Add the raspberries and mix gently.

■ Pour into the muffin cases and bake for 20 minutes. Cool slightly and then gently take the cakes out of the tin. Lightly dust the tops with icing sugar.

These are quite delicate, so use a flexible 8-hole muffin tin (the rubbery ones), or line a rigid tin with paper cases.

Double-chocolate almond biscotti

50 minutes ■ Makes about 50

plain flour 200g, plus extra for shaping dough

cocoa powder 60g

caster sugar 150g

dark chocolate 60g, chopped

baking powder ¾ tsp

salt ½ tsp

eggs 3, beaten

vanilla extract 1 tsp

blanched almonds 100g, toasted

white chocolate 100g, chopped

■ Heat the oven to 180C/fan 160C/gas 4. Put the flour, cocoa, sugar, dark chocolate, baking powder and salt into a food processor. Pulse until pulverised. Add the eggs and vanilla and pulse until a dough forms. Tip the dough onto a worksurface dusted with flour and knead in the nuts. Divide into four and shape into 2.5cm wide x 30cm flat logs. Lift them onto a paper-lined baking sheet. Bake for 25 minutes. Cool.

■ Use a serrated knife to diagonally cut the baked dough into 1.5cm pieces. Put on a baking sheet and cook for 15 minutes.

■ Cool on a wire rack. Melt the white chocolate in the microwave or a heatproof bowl set over a small pan of simmering water and drizzle over the biscotti. Store for up to 10 days in an airtight container.

Spiced brownies

50 minutes ■ Makes 12

butter 250g

cocoa powder 80g

golden granulated sugar 200g

dark muscovado sugar 200g

eggs 3

vanilla extract 1 tsp

plain flour 140g

mixed spice 1 tbsp

ground cloves a pinch

ground cinnamon 1 tsp

red chilli 1, deseeded and finely chopped

dark chocolate 100g (at least 50% cocoa solids), roughly chopped

■ Heat the oven to 180C/fan 160C/gas 4. Melt the butter and combine with the cocoa and sugars. Add the eggs and vanilla extract and mix again. Sift in the flour and spices and mix. Add the chilli and chocolate. Tip into a 20 x 30cm baking tray lined with foil and bake for 25–30 minutes until cooked but still slightly soft. Cool in the tin.

■ Turn out, peel off the foil and cut into 12 squares. Store wrapped in foil or clingfilm. Keeps for up to a week in a tin.

Rosemary and walnut shortbread

1 hour + chilling ■ Makes 30

plain flour 325g, plus extra for dusting
salted butter 200g
golden caster sugar 125g
eggs 2 yolks
rosemary 2 tsp, finely chopped
walnuts 60g, chopped

■ Put the flour and butter in a food processor and whizz until the mixture looks like breadcrumbs. Add the sugar, egg yolks and rosemary and whizz to a dough. Tip onto a lightly floured worksurface and knead in the walnuts. Shape into a log about 5cm across. Wrap in plastic and chill for an hour.
■ Heat the oven to 180C/fan 160C/gas 4. Slice the dough into biscuits and arrange on a buttered baking sheet. Bake for 20 minutes, then cool.

Chunky chocolate cookies

1 hour ■ Makes 18

plain flour 100g

bicarbonate of soda ¼ tsp

baking powder ¼ tsp

salt ¼ tsp

unsalted butter 125g

soft brown sugar 175g

golden caster sugar 25g

egg 1

vanilla extract 1 tsp

walnuts 50g, chopped

porridge oats 175g

dark chocolate 50g, chopped into
small chunks

■ Heat the oven to 180C/fan 160C/gas 4.
Mix the flour, bicarbonate of soda, baking
powder and salt in a bowl. Cream the butter,
sugars, egg and vanilla with electric beaters.
Stir in the flour mixture, then add the nuts,
oats and chocolate.

■ Line 2 baking sheets with non-stick baking
parchment and drop large tablespoons
of dough onto them. Press down gently.
Bake for 8–10 minutes until pale golden.
Let cool for 5 minutes before transferring
to a wire rack.

Chocolate and vanilla melting moments

50 minutes ■ Makes 16

unsalted butter 350g, softened

icing sugar 80g

vanilla extract 1 tsp

plain flour 300g

cornflour 50g

cocoa powder 25g

FILLING

mascarpone 250g

golden caster sugar 1 tbsp

dark chocolate 25g

vanilla extract a few drops

■ Heat the oven to 180C/fan 160C/gas 4. Beat the butter and icing sugar together until pale and creamy, then add the vanilla extract and mix well. Sift the flour and cornflour over and mix thoroughly. Halve the mixture and add the cocoa to one half. Mix well and add a drop of water if the mixture is too stiff.

■ Spoon the mixtures into 2 piping bags fitted with star nozzles. Line 2 baking sheets with baking parchment and pipe out 16 walnut-sized biscuits from each mixture, leaving a little space between each biscuit. Bake for 15–20 minutes or until cooked. Remove from the oven and allow to cool on the baking sheets.

■ Meanwhile, mix the mascarpone and sugar until smooth, then divide between 2 bowls. Melt the chocolate in a heatproof bowl over a pan of simmering water or in the microwave. Add the melted chocolate to one of the bowls and the vanilla to the other. Mix both until smooth.

■ Sandwich together the vanilla melting moments with the chocolate mascarpone and then the chocolate biscuits with the vanilla mascarpone.

Cupcakes

1 hour ■ Makes 20

unsalted butter 125g, softened
golden caster sugar 125g
orange 1, zested
eggs 2, beaten
plain flour 225g
baking powder 1 tsp
milk 100ml
BUTTERCREAM
unsalted butter 125g
icing sugar 3 tbsp, sifted, plus extra to dust
vanilla extract 1 tsp
food colouring (optional)
sugar flowers to decorate (optional)

■ Heat the oven to 180C/fan 160C/gas 4. Line two 12-hole cake tins with paper cases. Cream the butter and caster sugar together with an electric whisk until really pale and fluffy. Add the orange zest. Gradually add the beaten egg, mixing well between each addition. Sift together the flour and baking powder and fold into the creamed mixture. Add the milk and stir until smooth.

■ Divide the mixture between the paper cases and bake for about 20–25 minutes until golden and a skewer pushed in the middle comes out clean. Cool in the tins for 5 minutes and then transfer to a wire rack.

■ To make the buttercream, beat together the butter, icing sugar and vanilla extract (if you want coloured icing, beat in a drop of colouring). Spread over the top of the cooled cakes. Decorate with sugar flowers, if you like.

Chocolate fairy cakes

30 minutes ■ Makes 12

unsalted butter 150g, softened

golden caster sugar 150g

eggs 2 large, lightly beaten

vanilla extract 1 tsp

self-raising flour 115g

cocoa powder 35g

baking powder ½ rounded tsp

milk 3–4 tbsp

TOPPING

dark chocolate 75g

double cream 2 tbsp

unsalted butter 25g

icing sugar ½ tbsp

white chocolate 100g

glacé cherries 12

■ Heat the oven to 190C/Fan 170C/gas 5. Put 12 paper cases in a small cake tin. Beat the butter and caster sugar until it is light and fluffy. Gradually add the eggs and vanilla and mix well. Stir in the flour, cocoa, baking powder and a pinch of salt. Add enough milk to make the mixture drop easily from a spoon. Divide between the paper cases and bake for 20 minutes. Cool out of the tin.

■ Meanwhile, melt the plain chocolate with the cream, butter and icing sugar in a heatproof bowl set over a pan of simmering water or in a microwave, stirring until smooth. Leave to cool and thicken slightly, then ice the cakes. Melt the white chocolate, pour it into a plastic sandwich bag and twist closed. Snip off a tiny bit of a corner and drizzle the chocolate across the cakes. Top each cake with a cherry.

Carrot-cake muffins

1 hour 10 minutes ■ Makes 10

light muscovado sugar 100g
groundnut oil 75ml
unsalted butter 50g, melted
eggs 3
milk 2 tbsp
orange 1, zested
walnuts 75g, chopped
dates 75g, finely chopped
carrots 175g, coarsely grated
self-raising flour 175g
baking powder 1 tsp
ground cinnamon ½ tsp
FROSTING
cream cheese 300g
clear honey 2 tbsp
orange 1, zest finely grated

■ Heat the oven to 200C/fan 180C/gas 6. Line a regular muffin tin with 10 paper cases or strips of baking parchment. Put the sugar, oil, melted butter, eggs and milk in a bowl and whisk until smooth. Add the orange zest, walnuts, dates and carrots and mix. Sift the flour, baking powder and cinnamon together, and lightly fold into the muffin mixture. Do not overmix the batter as it should be slightly lumpy. Divide the mixture between the paper cases.

■ Bake for about 20–25 minutes until a skewer comes out clean. Cool in the tins and then transfer to a wire rack until completely cold. To make the frosting, beat together the cream cheese, honey and orange zest, and spread on top of each muffin.

Fondant fancies

1 hour 30 minutes ■ Makes 16–20

unsalted butter 250g, softened

golden caster sugar 250g

eggs 4, beaten

plain flour 250g

baking powder 2 tsp

milk 200ml, at room temperature

ground almonds 50g

vanilla extract 1 tsp

TO COVER

apricot jam 2 tbsp

marzipan 500g pack

icing sugar for rolling

fondant icing sugar 500g pack

food colouring, silver balls, edible sparkles to decorate

■ Heat the oven to 180C/fan 160C/gas 4. Butter a 30 x 23 x 4cm baking tin and line with greased baking parchment.

■ Cream the softened butter and caster sugar until light and fluffy. Gradually mix in the beaten eggs. Sift together the flour and baking powder, fold one-third into the creamed mixture. Mix in one-third of the milk. Add the remaining flour and milk in alternate batches to the mixture. Fold in the almonds and vanilla extract, stir until smooth then spoon into the tin.

■ Spread level and bake for about 40 minutes or until a skewer inserted into the middle of the cake comes out clean. Remove from the oven and cool in the tin.

■ Melt the apricot jam and sieve. Remove the cake from the tin and brush the top with the jam. Roll the marzipan out to a rectangle the same size as the cake, lay on top of the jam and smooth the surface. Trim the sides of the cake and cut into 4cm squares.

■ Mix the fondant icing sugar with cold water until smooth and thick enough to coat the cakes. Divide into batches and colour as you like, using food colouring. Coat each cake with icing and dry on a wire rack.

■ Pipe thin lines or rosettes in contrasting colours and decorate with silver balls and edible sparkles.

Blueberry and white chocolate muffins

40 minutes ■ Makes 6

plain flour 150g

golden caster sugar 50g

baking powder ½ tsp

egg 1, beaten

butter 50g, melted and cooled

milk 100ml

blueberries 75g

white chocolate 75g, chopped into chunks

■ Heat the oven to 200C/fan 180C/gas 6 and line a 6-hole muffin tin with paper cases. Mix the flour, sugar and baking powder with a pinch of salt. Mix the egg, melted butter and milk quickly into the dry ingredients with the blueberries and chocolate (don't overmix, it should be a bit lumpy). Divide between the cases and bake for 25 minutes until risen and golden and cooked through.

Chocolate marble meringues

1 hour 30 minutes ■ Makes 12

....

dark chocolate 100g

egg whites 4

lemon 1, halved

golden caster sugar 200g

whipping cream 284ml carton, whipped

■ Heat the oven to 120C/fan 100C/gas ½. Melt the chocolate in a microwave or in a heatproof bowl set over a pan of simmering water, then leave to cool a little. The chocolate needs to be liquid enough to pour slowly.

■ Whisk the egg whites with a squeeze of lemon juice until they form stiff peaks, then beat in the sugar a little at a time until you have a stiff, shiny meringue. Spoon the meringue mixture into a piping bag and, using a wooden spoon handle, make a hole in the mixture all the way to the funnel tip. Pour the chocolate into the hole.

■ Pipe meringues about 6–7cm across, spaced well apart, on baking sheets lined with baking paper; the chocolate will swirl out and marble the meringue as you pipe.

■ Bake for 1 hour or until set, then switch off the oven and leave them inside to cool. Sandwich 2 together with the cream to serve.

Cherry and almond muffins

40 minutes ■ Makes 12

golden caster sugar 150g, plus a little more to sprinkle on top

vanilla extract 1 tsp

egg 1

butter 125g, melted

Greek yoghurt 175ml

plain flour 200g

baking powder 1 tsp

ground almonds 100g

cherries 250g, pitted and halved

■ Heat the oven to 180C/fan 160C/gas 4. Line a 12-hole muffin tin with muffin cases (not cupcake ones as these are too small). Mix the sugar, vanilla, egg, butter and yoghurt.

■ Sift the flour, baking powder and almonds into a bowl (use a wide-mesh sieve), add the liquid ingredients and mix quickly (don't worry if the mix is lumpy), add the cherries and mix. Divide between the muffin cases, sprinkle a little extra sugar onto each and bake for 20 minutes or until risen and golden.

Passion fruit friands

30 minutes ■ Makes 20

unsalted butter 180g, melted and cooled

eggs 5 whites

self-raising flour 75g

icing sugar 200g

ground almonds 125g

passion fruit 4, pulp scooped out or 150g tin of pulp

caster sugar 2 tbsp

■ Heat the oven to 200C/fan 180C/gas 6. Butter 2 x 12-hole muffin tins (or line them with paper cases, if you prefer).

■ Whisk the egg whites until they hold a soft peak.

■ Sift the flour, icing sugar and almonds over the whisked egg whites and pour the melted butter around the edge of the bowl. Fold together very gently and spoon into 20 of the holes. Bake for 15 minutes or until the friands are risen and golden – they should feel slightly springy to the touch.

■ Mix the passion fruit and caster sugar and spoon over the warm friands in the tins. Leave for 5 minutes and then lift out of the tins and cool on a wire rack.

Sunday morning cakes

45 minutes + rising ■ Makes 16

milk 250ml

butter 150g

golden caster sugar 250g

fast-action dried yeast 7g sachet

eggs 3, beaten

plain flour 550g, sifted

cinnamon 1 tsp

soured cream 1 tbsp

TOPPING

icing sugar 125g

lemon 1, juiced

■ Heat the milk to just below boiling point, add the butter, 130g of the sugar and a pinch of salt. Stir and cool a little. Add the yeast and stir until dissolved. Add the eggs, then enough flour to make a pillowy dough. Knead well on a floured surface. Put into a buttered bowl and leave to rise in a warm place until doubled in size. Halve and shape into 2 large, flat oblongs.

■ Mix the rest of the sugar with the cinnamon and soured cream. Spread over the dough and then roll each lengthways to make 2 long Swiss rolls. Pinch the edges firmly together. Now either cut each roll into fat slices or keep them whole and slash their tops. Allow to rise again and double in size, about 30 minutes.

■ Heat the oven to 190C/fan 170C/gas 5. Bake for 25 minutes (longer if you're making them as loaves) or until golden and risen. Before the pastry has cooled completely, mix the icing sugar and lemon juice into a paste and brush over.

Toffee apple and pecan muffins

45 minutes ■ Makes 12

butter 100g, melted and cooled
eggs 2, beaten
milk 100ml
soured cream 150ml
plain flour 300g
golden caster sugar 100g
baking powder 2 tsp
bicarbonate of soda 1 tsp
apples 3 small (about 300g), peeled, cored and diced
pecans 50g, roughly chopped
soft toffees 100g, chopped

■ Heat the oven to 200C/fan 180C/gas 6 and line a 12-hole muffin tin with paper cases. Mix the wet ingredients quickly into the dry ingredients with the apples, pecans and toffees (don't overmix – it should be a bit lumpy). Divide between the cases and bake for 25 minutes until risen, golden and cooked through.

Pineapple upside-down cakelets

40 minutes ■ Serves 8

pineapple rings in natural juice 220g can, drained

butter 150g, melted

maraschino cherries or **glacé cherries** 8

golden syrup 250ml

eggs 4

caster sugar 125g

lemon 1, grated zest only

self-raising flour 100g

■ Heat the oven to 200C/fan 180C/gas 6. Put a pineapple ring in the bottom of 8 buttered 200ml ramekins or small soufflé dishes, then put a cherry in the middle of each ring. Add a generous spoonful or two of golden syrup to each of the ramekins.

■ Whisk the eggs and sugar with an electric whisk until very thick, pale and fluffy – this will take about 10 minutes. Beat in the butter and lemon zest. Sift over the flour and fold it in carefully. Divide evenly between the dishes.

■ Bake for 20–25 minutes until the cakelets are firm to the touch and the syrup is beginning to bubble up around the edges. Turn out onto plates and serve straight away, or leave to cool in their dishes. To reheat, cover the dishes with foil and put back into a 200C/fan 180C/gas 6 oven for 10–15 minutes.

Lime and coconut angel cakes with passion fruit

1 hour 30 minutes ■ Serves 6

eggs 7 whites
lime zest of 1 plus 2 tsp juice
cream of tartar ¾ tsp (look in the baking section of supermarkets)
caster sugar 120g
plain flour 60g
cornflour 15g
desiccated coconut 50g
passion fruit 4 large

■ Heat the oven to 160C/fan 140C/gas 3. Whisk the egg whites with a pinch of salt and the lime juice until foamy. Add the cream of tartar and continue to whisk until stiff but not dry. Gradually whisk in 90g caster sugar with the lime zest (reserving some to sprinkle over the baked cakes) until it forms a thick and glossy meringue.

■ Sift the remaining caster sugar and the flours into a bowl and fold into the meringue in 3 batches to retain as much air as possible. Fold in the desiccated coconut. Spoon into 6 unoiled 10cm bundt tins and bake for 30 minutes, until firm and pale golden on top.

■ Turn the tins upside down on a wire rack (this creates steam to loosen the cakes) and leave for 10 minutes. Give each cake a very firm shake and a tap to release them then cool completely on the wire rack.

■ Scoop out the passion fruit pulp and push through a sieve to remove the seeds. Drizzle the juice over the finished cakes and sprinkle with the reserved lime zest before serving.

Breakfast muffins

40 minutes ■ Makes 6

....

oil 100ml (use any oil without much flavour)
wholemeal flour 125g, sifted
plain flour 125g, sifted
baking powder 2 tsp
molasses sugar or other dark sugar 100g
pumpkin seeds a handful, plus a few extra
for the tops
sultanas or **raisins,** a handful
bananas 4, very ripe and mashed
(or 350ml thick fruit purée)
eggs 2, lightly beaten
milk 2 tbsp

■ Heat the oven to 180C/fan 160C/gas 4.
Line 6 holes of an greased non-stick muffin
tin with squares of baking paper (cut a
square and push it in so it comes up the sides
to the top of the tin). Mix the flours, baking
powder, sugar, seeds and sultanas in a bowl,
then add the oil, bananas, eggs and milk. Fold
quickly with a large metal spoon and don't
worry if the mix is still lumpy – mixing for too
long makes muffins tough.

■ Divide the mixture between muffin tins. Fill
them to the top, sprinkle on a few extra seeds
and bake for 20 minutes or until the muffins
are cooked through. Cool briefly, then put on
a wire rack.

Raspberry and white chocolate macaroons

50 minutes ■ Makes about 25

icing sugar 275g
ground almonds 120g
powdered egg white 8g sachet
egg whites 85g (you'll need 2–3 eggs)
pink food colouring
seedless raspberry jam 3 tbsp
GANACHE
white chocolate 75g
butter 15g
double cream 75ml

■ To make the ganache, melt the chocolate and butter together in a microwave or in a heatproof bowl set over a pan of simmering water. Lightly whip the cream and fold in. Cover and set aside.

■ Line 2 baking sheets with non-stick baking parchment and heat the oven to 160C/fan 140C/gas 3. Sift the icing sugar and almonds into a bowl. Use a food processor to re-grind any almond pieces left in the sieve to a fine powder.

■ In a separate bowl, whisk the powdered egg white and fresh egg whites to stiff peaks. Add the colouring, a tiny amount at a time, to get a soft pink. Fold the almond mixture in – the volume will deflate massively.

■ Transfer to a piping bag and pipe rounds of the mixture onto the baking sheets. They will spread a little as you pipe, but each macaroon should be about 5cm in diameter. Cook for about 12–15 minutes, until risen with a frilly base but not coloured. Watch them and if they start to turn golden, reduce the oven temperature.

■ Carefully loosen each macaroon. If they stick to the baking sheets, pour a little water under the baking parchment, being careful not to get the macaroons wet. Leave for a minute to steam them off from underneath, then leave to cool.

■ Spread a macaroon with a little ganache and another with raspberry jam. Sandwich together and leave for 15 minutes, to soften the macaroons slightly, and serve. Filled macaroons will keep in an airtight container for up to 12 hours.

Lemon and poppy seed shortcakes

40 minutes ■ Makes 8

plain flour 325g
baking powder 1 tbsp
caster sugar 4 tbsp
unsalted butter 125g, diced and chilled
poppy seeds 1 tbsp
unwaxed lemon 1, zested
egg 1, beaten
double cream 125ml, plus 2 tbsp
VANILLA CREAM
vanilla pod 1, seeds scraped out
icing sugar 2 tbsp
double cream 300ml
ripe peaches 6
caster sugar 2 tbsp
lemon 2 tbsp juice

■ Heat the oven to 220C/fan 200C/gas 7. Put the flour, a pinch of salt, baking powder and 3 tbsp caster sugar into a food processor. Add the butter, poppy seeds and lemon zest. Using the pulse button, rub the butter into the dry ingredients.

■ Tip into a large bowl, add the beaten egg and 125ml double cream and, using a knife, stir until the dough comes together.

■ Lightly flour the worksurface and roll the dough out to about 3cm. Dip a 7cm cutter into flour and then stamp out as many shortcakes from the dough as you can. Re-roll the scraps and stamp out more shortcakes to make 8 in total. Arrange on a parchment-lined baking sheet, brush the tops with a little double cream and sprinkle with the caster sugar. Bake for about 15 minutes or until well-risen and golden brown. Cool slightly.

■ To make the vanilla cream, softly whip the vanilla seeds, icing sugar and cream in a bowl. Cover and chill until needed. Slice the peaches and mix with the caster sugar and lemon juice. Split the warm shortcakes in half, add a good dollop of vanilla cream, some peaches and put the top back on. Serve immediately.

Orange and carrot muffins

45 minutes ■ Makes 12

plain flour 300g
baking powder 2 tsp
caster sugar 100g
cinnamon ½ tsp
egg 1, beaten
butter 75g, melted
oranges 2, zested and juiced
carrots 100g, peeled and grated

■ Heat the oven to 190C/fan 170C/gas 5. Line a 12-hole muffin tin with squares of baking parchment, pushing them down to make little cases. Mix the flour, baking powder, sugar and cinnamon with ½ tsp salt.

■ Whisk together the egg, melted butter, orange zest and juice with the carrots, then stir this into the dry ingredients, but don't overmix – it's better if it's a bit lumpy. Spoon into the muffin tin and bake for 20–25 minutes until risen.

Ginger madeleines

30 minutes + chilling ■ Makes 12 large
or 36 small

plain flour 100g, plus extra for dusting
baking powder ½ tsp
ground ginger 1 tsp
golden caster sugar 75g
eggs 2
vanilla extract 1 tsp
stem ginger 2 pieces from a jar, finely
chopped, plus 1 tbsp of the ginger syrup
unsalted butter 90g, melted, plus extra
for greasing
icing sugar 1 tbsp

■ Sift the flour, baking powder and ground
ginger together with a pinch of salt. Whisk
the sugar and eggs with electric beaters until
they are thick and fluffy. Gently fold in the
flour mix, vanilla and stem ginger and syrup.
Then fold in the butter. Cover the surface of
the mix with clingfilm and chill for 30 minutes.
■ Heat the oven to 200C/fan 180C/gas 6.
Butter 12 ordinary madeleine tins or 36 mini
ones and dust with flour. Fill each with a large
blob of mixture (1 heaped tbsp for a large
mould). Bake for 10 minutes (minis will need
6) or until risen, golden and springy. Tap the
tin to loosen, and tip out. Dust with icing
sugar and serve warm.

Layer cakes with strawberry buttercream

1 hour 30 minutes ■ Makes 6

eggs 6

golden caster sugar 150g

vanilla extract 1 tsp

plain flour 125g, sifted

unsalted butter 3 tbsp, melted

raspberry or **strawberry liqueur** 2–3 tbsp

STRAWBERRY BUTTERCREAM

unsalted butter 125g, softened

icing sugar 500g

strawberries 4, hulled and chopped

strawberries and **redcurrants** to decorate

■ Heat the oven to 180C/fan 160C/gas 4. Line a 23 x 30cm Swiss roll tin with baking paper. Beat the eggs, sugar, a pinch of salt and the vanilla until tripled in volume, about 8–10 minutes. Fold in the flour and butter in batches. Spread evenly in the tin and bake for 25 minutes. Cool in the tin, remove and peel off the paper. Cut out twelve 6cm or 7cm rings using a cutter. Slice each in half lengthways and brush all over with liqueur.

■ To make the buttercream, whisk the butter in a bowl using an electric hand whisk then gradually mix in the icing sugar. Add the strawberries and whisk until finely chopped (the icing will turn pink). Ice one side of each disc and stack to make 6 cakes, each with 4 layers. Ice the outsides and top with fruit.

Chocolate fondant fancies

1 hour 15 minutes ■ Makes 25

plain flour 175g
baking powder 1 tsp
butter 175g, softened
golden caster sugar 175g
eggs 3, lightly beaten
cocoa powder 1 large tbsp
dark chocolate truffles 13 small round
ones, halved
ICING
dark chocolate 100g
butter 25g
icing sugar 6 tbsp
milk chocolate 50g, melted, to decorate

■ Heat the oven to 160C/fan 140C/gas 3. Put the flour, baking powder, butter, caster sugar, eggs and cocoa powder into a large bowl and beat together with an electric whisk. The mixture should drop easily from a spoon – add a little water if it's too stiff. Spoon the mix into a 23cm square cake tin (try to use one without rounded edges).

■ Bake for 30–35 minutes or until the cake is cooked through (test with a skewer). Remove from the tin and cool completely. Cut into 25 squares. Top each square with half a truffle, cut-side down.

■ To make the icing, melt the plain chocolate and butter together with 4 tbsp water in a microwave or a heatproof bowl set over a pan of simmering water. Mix in the icing sugar. Spoon over the top of the cakes, spreading round the sides and over the truffle with a small palette knife. If the icing gets too thick, heat it up slightly. Leave the dark icing to set for a few minutes, then drizzle the milk chocolate over with a teaspoon.

Clementine and poppy seed muffins

45 minutes ■ Makes 12

self-raising flour 250g
baking powder 2 tsp
golden caster sugar 100g
poppy seeds 2 tbsp
clementines 4 zested, 3 juiced
butter 100g, melted
eggs 2, beaten
natural yoghurt 200ml

■ Heat the oven to 180C/fan 160C/gas 4 and line a 12-hole muffin tin with paper cases. Put the flour, baking powder, sugar and poppy seeds in a large bowl with a pinch of salt and mix together.

■ In another bowl, whisk the remaining ingredients together and pour into the bowl with the other ingredients. Mix together quickly (don't overmix, you want it a bit lumpy). Divide between the paper cases and bake for 25–30 minutes until risen and golden.

Frosted lemon fairy cakes

50 minutes ■ Makes 12

golden caster sugar 125g

unsalted butter 125g, at room temperature

lemons 2, zested plus 4 tbsp juice

eggs 2

self-raising flour 125g

icing sugar 185g, sifted

LEMON SUGAR TOPPING

golden caster sugar 100g

lemon 1, zested

■ To make the lemon sugar topping, whizz 50g golden caster sugar in a food processor with most of the lemon zest, then mix in the remaining sugar. Tip onto a baking sheet and leave to dry for 1 hour.

■ To make the cakes, heat the oven to 180C/fan 160C/gas 4. Beat the sugar, butter and lemon zest using an electric mixer until light and fluffy – give it plenty of time as this will make the cakes nice and light. Add 1 egg at a time with a spoonful of the flour to prevent curdling.

■ Finally, mix in the remaining flour and 2 tbsp lemon juice. Line a bun tin with 12 cases and divide the mix between them. Bake for 18–20 minutes, until risen and light golden. Cool on a wire rack.

■ Mix the icing sugar and remaining 2 tbsp lemon juice until smooth. Remove the paper cases from the cakes and sit on wire racks. Ice the tops of the cakes. Sprinkle with lemon sugar and the remaining zest and leave to set.

Nutmeg and bay custard tarts

1 hour 45 minutes ■ Makes 6

....

shortcrust pastry 500g
eggs 4, 3 separated
golden caster sugar 1 tbsp
single cream 284ml carton
whole nutmeg 1
bay leaves 6 small

■ Heat the oven to 200C/fan 180C/gas 6. Roll out the pastry to the thickness of a 20p coin and line 6 deep 10cm tart tins. Then line each one with foil and baking beans and bake for about 10 minutes or until the pastry looks cooked.

■ Take out the beans and foil and bake for another couple of minutes to dry the base of the pastry. Brush the insides with a little egg white. Turn down the oven to 150C/fan 130C/gas 2.

■ Mix the whole egg and 3 separated yolks with the sugar. Bring the cream almost up to the boil and then whisk it into the yolks. Grate in a good pinch of nutmeg. Put the tart tins on a baking sheet and carefully pour in the custard mixture. Grate over a little more nutmeg and float a bay leaf on each. Bake for about 30 minutes or until the custard has set.

Make meringues with the leftover egg whites. Whisk to firm peaks then add 2 tbsp sugar per egg white. Whisk until stiff and glossy then spoon onto a baking tray and bake in a low oven until crisp.

Chocolate and ginger tart

1 hour ■ Serves 8

white chocolate 200g

liquid glucose 3 tbsp (from supermarkets and chemists)

dark chocolate 200g

double cream 284ml carton

stem ginger from a jar 4 lumps, finely chopped, plus 2 tbsp of the syrup

PASTRY

plain flour 150g

cocoa powder 20g

unsalted butter 75g, chilled and cubed

golden caster sugar 3 tbsp

egg yolks 3

vanilla extract a few drops

■ To make the pastry, put the flour, cocoa and butter in a food processor and whizz to fine crumbs using the pulse button. Whizz in the sugar and then add the egg yolks and vanilla and process briefly to make a paste. Shape into a disc, wrap in clingfilm and chill.

■ Heat the oven to 180C/fan 160C/gas 4. Roll the pastry out and line a deep 20cm-diameter tart tin. Bake blind for 15 minutes or until the pastry is very dry. Cool. Melt half of the white chocolate in the microwave or in a heatproof bowl over a pan of simmering water and paint it over the base of the tart. Cool.

■ Melt the glucose and dark chocolate together in a pan over a low heat. Transfer to a bowl and cool slightly. Lightly whip the cream and fold into the chocolate, then fold in the ginger and syrup and spoon into the tart. Chill until set.

■ Melt the remaining white chocolate and pour it into a piping bag (or use a freezer bag and snip off a corner). Draw a swirl of chocolate onto the top of the tart. Wait for it to set before cutting with a hot knife.

Jam tarts

45 minutes + chilling ■ Makes 24

....

unsalted butter 150g, cold
plain flour 250g, plus extra for rolling
icing sugar 1 tbsp
egg yolks 2
raspberry, strawberry, blackcurrant and
apricot jam

■ Dice the butter and put in a food processor
with the plain flour and icing sugar. Pulse
until the butter has been incorporated into
the flour and the mixture resembles fine
breadcrumbs or rub the butter into the flour
and sugar with your hands.

■ Add the egg yolks and 2 tbsp ice-cold water
and pulse again until the pastry begins to
come together. Gather the dough into a ball,
flatten into a disc, wrap in clingfilm and chill
for 30 minutes.

■ Heat the oven to 200C/fan 180C/gas 6.
Roll the pastry out on a lightly floured
worksurface, and using a 7cm cutter stamp
out 24 discs.

■ Line two 12-hole mini tart tins with the
pastry discs. Fill each pastry case with 2 tsp
jam and bake for about 15 minutes or until
the pastry is crisp and golden.

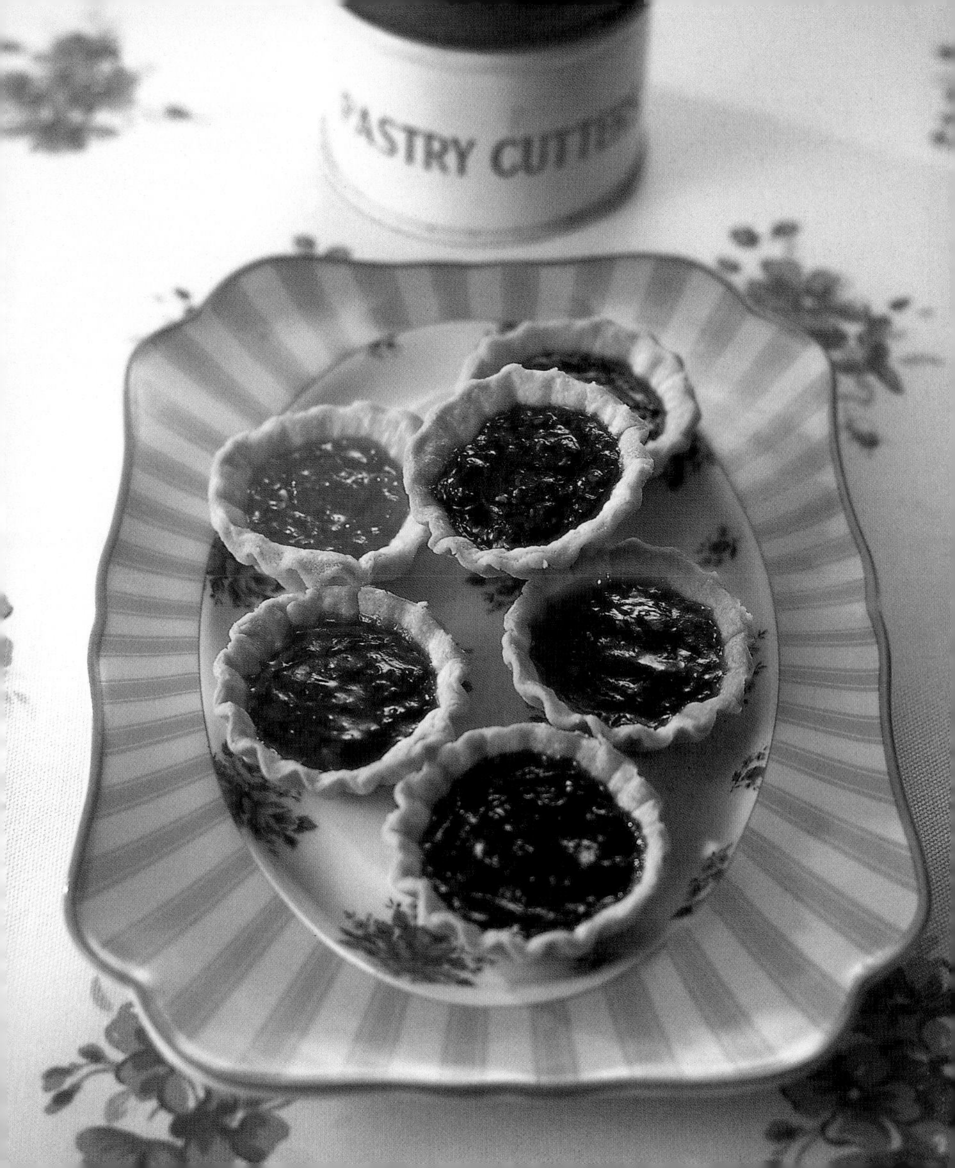
ASTRY CUTTE

Toffee banana puffs with chantilly cream

40 minutes ■ Serves 4

bananas 4 small
ready-rolled puff pastry 2 sheets
egg 1, beaten
unrefined demerara sugar
double cream 284ml carton
icing sugar
vanilla extract a few drops

■ Heat the oven to 200C/fan 180C/gas 6. Slice the bananas in half horizontally.

■ Unroll the pastry and lay the banana halves on top, cut-side up. Cut around each half, leaving a 2cm border. Put the banana pastries on a baking sheet and brush the borders with egg. Sprinkle the tops of the bananas with demerara sugar.

■ Bake for 15–20 minutes until the pastry is puffed and golden and the bananas are caramelised. Softly whip the cream, icing sugar and vanilla together. Serve 2 puffs per person with a dollop of cream.

Lime tart

1 hour 10 minutes ■ Serves 8

shortcrust pastry 350g, fresh or frozen
eggs 6 (4 whole, 2 separated)
caster sugar 150g
limes 6, zested and juiced, make some
curls of zest from 1 lime for decoration,
if you like
double cream 142ml carton
icing sugar

■ Heat the oven to 200C/fan 180C/gas 6. Line a 22cm loose-bottomed tart tin or tart ring with the pastry, rolling it as thin as you can. Line with baking parchment and baking weights and bake blind for 10 minutes, then lift out the parchment and bake for a further 5 minutes or until the pastry base looks dry and golden brown. Turn the oven down to 160C/fan 140C/gas 3.

■ Whisk the 4 whole eggs, the 2 yolks and the caster sugar together. Stir in the lime zest and juice and the cream. Pour into the pastry case and cook for 30–40 minutes or until the filling is just set. Cool. Dust with icing sugar. Serve each slice with a curl of lime.

Bakewell tart

1 hour 30 minutes + chilling ■ Serves 8

PASTRY
plain flour 125g
unsalted butter 75g, cold and diced
caster sugar 25g
egg 1, separated
FILLING
raspberry jam 2 heaped tbsp
unsalted butter 150g, at room
temperature
caster sugar 150g
eggs 3, beaten
egg yolk 1
ground almonds 150g
lemon 1, zested
flaked almonds 1 tbsp
cream or **custard** to serve

■ To make the pastry, tip the flour, butter and sugar into a food processor with a pinch of salt. Whizz until the mixture resembles breadcrumbs. Add the egg yolk and 1 tsp of cold water and pulse until the dough comes together. Flatten into a disc, cover with clingfilm and chill for no more than 1 hour. Roll out the pastry on a lightly floured surface to about 3mm thickness. Line a 20cm fluted tart tin with a depth of 3½cm. Prick the base with a fork and chill for 20 minutes.

■ Heat the oven to 180C/fan 160C/gas 4. Line the pastry case with baking parchment and fill with baking beans. Cook for about 20 minutes until the pastry is a pale golden colour. Take out the beans, brush the inside of the pastry case with a little egg white and cook for a further 2 minutes. Cool slightly.

■ Spread the jam in an even layer over the base of the pastry case. Cream together the butter and caster sugar. Gradually add the beaten eggs and egg yolk. Fold in the ground almonds and lemon zest. Carefully spoon the mixture over the jam and spread level. Bake for 20 minutes. Scatter with the flaked almonds and continue to cook for a further 15–20 minutes until golden and set.

■ Cool to room temperature and serve with pouring cream or custard.

Banana and ginger Tatins

30 minutes ■ Makes 6

golden caster sugar 200g
ready-rolled puff pastry 375g pack
root ginger 1cm piece, peeled and finely grated
bananas 4 large, thinly sliced
milk 2 tsp
vanilla ice cream or **crème fraîche** to serve

■ Heat the oven to 220C/fan 200C/gas 7. To make the caramel sauce, dissolve the sugar in a heavy-based pan with 60ml water, then boil rapidly for about 5–7 minutes until it starts to turn golden. Remove from the heat – it will continue to colour.

■ Cut 6 circles measuring 10cm each out of the pastry. Put a pinch of ginger into 6 holes of a Yorkshire pudding tin. Spoon some caramel sauce on top, then cover with the banana slices and top with a pastry circle.

■ Press the pastry gently into the tins. Brush with some milk and bake for about 20 minutes until crisp and golden. Invert onto a serving plate while the caramel is still hot (use a spatula to help you hoick out any banana that gets stuck). Serve with vanilla ice cream or crème fraîche.

Strawberry and crème fraîche tart

45 minutes + chilling ■ Serves 6

sweet shortcrust pastry 350g

orange 1, zest grated

crème fraîche 500ml

Cointreau 2 tbsp (or Grand Marnier)

caster sugar 3 tbsp

whipping cream 142ml, chilled

strawberries 250g, stalks pulled out

lavender sugar (optional)

■ Heat the oven to 200C/fan 180C/gas 6. Roll out the pastry until big enough to line an 18–20cm loose-bottomed tart tin (or cake tin). Scatter over the orange zest and press in lightly. Line the tart tin with pastry, then cover with a piece of foil or baking paper.

■ Weigh down with baking beans, pushing them towards the edges of the tin. Bake for 15 minutes, until set, then remove the paper or foil and weights and bake for a further 5 minutes until lightly coloured. Allow to cool.

■ Beat the crème fraîche, Cointreau and caster sugar together. Whip the cream to soft peaks and fold into the mixture. Pour into the tart case, cover and chill for at least 1 hour and up to 8 hours.

■ Slice the strawberries in half and arrange on top of the tart. Dredge with lavender sugar, if using.

Toffee pear galettes

40 minutes ■ Makes 4

....

puff pastry 1 sheet of fresh or frozen ready-rolled, cut into 4 circles
dulce de leche 2 tbsp (or other toffee sauce)
pears 2 small ripe, halved, cored and thinly sliced to make a fan shape (leave joined at the stalk end)
egg 1, whisked to glaze
crème fraîche to serve

■ Heat the oven to 200C/fan 180C/gas 6. Lay the pastry on a baking sheet. Put ½ tbsp dulce de leche in the centre of each circle and fan a pear out on top.

■ Glaze the edges with egg then bake for 20–25 minutes or until puffed and golden. Serve with a dollop of crème fraîche.

Cardamom and pistachio twists

35 minutes ■ Makes 12

cardamom pods 15
caster sugar 5 tbsp
ready-rolled puff pastry 375g pack
shelled pistachios 50g, chopped
dark chocolate 50g, melted (optional)

Layering the sugar and pastry on these is a neat trick that helps make the pastry gorgeously crisp.

■ Heat the oven to 200C/fan 180C/gas 6. Break open the cardamom pods and tip out the seeds. Crush using a pestle and mortar, or in a bowl with the end of a rolling pin. Mix in 1 tbsp of sugar.

■ Sprinkle 1 tbsp of sugar on a worksurface, put the pastry on top and roll it out to twice its original length. Scatter over the cardamom sugar and run the rolling pin over the pastry again to press the sugar in.

■ Fold the pastry in half (so that it's back to its original size), sprinkle over another tbsp of sugar and roll it out again. Scatter over the pistachios and roll them in. Fold the pastry in half once more, scatter over 1 tbsp of sugar and give it a gentle roll to press it in.

■ Cut the pastry into 2cm-wide strips and give each one 2 twists. Put on a baking sheet and sprinkle with the remaining spoonful of sugar. Bake for about 15 minutes until browned and slightly shiny.

■ Cool on a wire rack, then – as an optional extra – drizzle with melted chocolate. Allow to set before serving.

Lemon and raspberry curd tarts

1 hour 30 minutes ■ Makes 8

sweet pastry 500g block

LEMON CURD

caster sugar 225g

unsalted butter 125g

unwaxed lemons 3, zested and juiced

eggs 2

egg yolk 1

RASPBERRY CURD

raspberries 300g, mashed and sieved

caster sugar 125g

unsalted butter 125g

eggs 2

egg yolks 2

lemon ½, juiced

■ Line eight 10cm tart tins with pastry rolled to the thickness of a £1 coin. Prick the bases and chill for 30 minutes.

■ Heat the oven to 200C/fan 180C/gas 6 and put a solid baking sheet in the oven. Blind-bake the tarts for 15–20 minutes then leave to cool completely.

■ To make the lemon curd, put the sugar, butter, lemon zest and juice in a heatproof bowl set over a pan of simmering water until the butter and sugar are melted. Whisk the whole eggs and egg yolk together and strain into the butter and lemon. Continue to cook until the curd coats the back of a spoon, then cool and chill.

■ To make the raspberry curd, put the mashed and sieved raspberries, caster sugar and butter in a bowl and put over a pan of simmering water. Stir occasionally until the sugar and butter have completely melted. Beat the whole eggs and yolks together and strain into the raspberry mixture. Continue to cook until the mixture coats the back of a spoon. Add a little lemon juice to taste and remove from heat. Cool completely before covering with clingfilm and chill until needed.

■ To serve, put a baked tart shell on each plate. Fill one half of the tart with lemon curd and the other half with raspberry. Swirl together with a skewer or the tip of a knife. Repeat with the remaining tarts and serve immediately.

Dark chocolate and salted caramel tart

1 hour 50 minutes ■ Serves 8

plain flour 200g

sugar 2 tbsp

cocoa 2 tbsp

butter 100g

egg yolks 2

vanilla extract a few drops

CARAMEL

sugar 250g

salted butter 125g

single cream 100ml

sea salt flakes a pinch

CHOCOLATE LAYER

sugar 2 tbsp

egg 1

egg yolk 1

dark chocolate 100g

unsalted butter 75g

■ To make the pastry, heat the oven to 200C/fan 180C/gas 6. Whizz the flour, sugar and cocoa in a processor. Add the butter and whizz until breadcrumbs. Add the egg yolks and vanilla extract, whizz to a dough. Press into a disc, wrap in clingfilm and chill for 30 minutes. Roll out the pastry and line a deep 20cm tart tin. Chill for 30 minutes.

■ To make the caramel, dissolve the sugar in 5 tbsp water in a large pan. Stir in the butter and simmer until it turns a light toffee colour. Turn off the heat and stir in the cream, then add a pinch of sea salt flakes. Leave to cool.

■ Prick the base of the tart with a fork. Scrunch a long piece of foil into a sausage, curl it into a circle and fit it inside the tart, pressing against the sides of the tart to hold them up as it cooks. Bake for 12 minutes. Turn the heat down to 190C/fan 170C/gas 5.

■ To make the chocolate layer, beat the sugar, egg and egg yolk together with an electric whisk until thick and custard coloured. Melt the chocolate and butter together, pour into the egg mixture and beat until smooth and glossy. Spread the caramel over the base of the tart. Spoon the chocolate mixture over the top, spreading it evenly. Bake for 12 minutes, then leave to cool in the tin.

Sugar crust cherry pie

1 hour 30 minutes ■ Serves 4

cherries 500g, stoned
caster sugar 2–3 tbsp
kirsch 1 tbsp
vanilla ice cream to serve
SWEET PASTRY
plain flour 400g
butter 200g, cold, diced
caster sugar 50g
egg yolks 2, plus 1 for glazing
demerara sugar 2 tbsp

■ Toss the cherries and sugar together with the kirsch and leave to macerate for 20 minutes.

■ To make the pastry, put the flour in a food processor, add the butter and pulse to breadcrumbs. Add the caster sugar and mix. Add the 2 egg yolks and pulse until the mixture comes together (you might need to add a splash of cold water as well). Wrap in clingfilm and chill for 20 minutes.

■ Heat the oven to 190C/fan 170C/gas 5. Roll out half the pastry and line 1 large or 4 small pie dishes. Put the cherry mixture in the bottom then roll out the rest of the pastry and drape over the top and trim. Crimp and seal the edges then glaze all over with the remaining egg yolk. Bake for 30–35 minutes until the pastry is crisp and golden.

■ In the last 5 minutes of cooking, sprinkle the demerara sugar over. Rest for 10 minutes before serving with vanilla ice cream.

Peach and almond tart

1 hour 30 minutes + chilling ■ Serves 8

sweet pastry 500g

egg white a little, to glaze

sweet wine 200ml

caster sugar 100g

lemon 1, juiced

peaches 4, cut into wedges

FRANGIPANE

blanched almonds 75g

blanched hazelnuts 100g

unsalted butter 150g, at room temperature

caster sugar 100g

eggs 3, beaten

plain flour 75g

lemon ½, zested

■ On a lightly floured surface, roll out the pastry to 3mm thick and line a rectangular 28 x 20cm or 24cm round fluted tart tin with a depth of 2.5cm. Lightly prick the base and chill for 20 minutes. Heat the oven to 180C/fan 160C/gas 4.

■ Blind-bake for 20 minutes or until the pastry is a pale golden colour. Remove the baking beans and brush the pastry case with a little egg white then return to the oven for a further 2 minutes. Remove and cool slightly.

■ Heat the wine, sugar, lemon juice and 100ml water in a wide pan over a medium heat to dissolve the sugar. Bring to the boil, reduce to a simmer and add the peach wedges. Poach for 10 minutes until tender. Remove and cool. Simmer the remaining syrup until it is reduced to about 6–8 tbsp.

■ To make the frangipane, finely chop the almonds and hazelnuts in the food processor and remove. Cream the butter and sugar in the food processor until pale. Gradually add the beaten eggs, mixing well between each addition. Fold in the nuts, flour and lemon zest and mix until smooth.

■ Tip the filling into the tart tin and level. Arrange the peaches on the top and slide the tart onto a baking sheet. Bake for about 30 minutes or until golden. Brush the warm tart with some of the syrup, cool, and then serve the rest of the syrup on the side.

Apple and blackberry pies

1 hour 15 minutes + chilling ■ Makes 12 mini pies

plain flour 300g, plus a little extra for rolling out
unsalted butter 150g, chilled and diced
icing sugar 2 level tbsp
egg yolk 1
ice-cold water 2–3 tbsp
FILLING
dessert apples 3, peeled, cored and diced
Bramley apples 1 large, peeled, cored and diced
golden caster sugar 25g
butter
lemon a squeeze of juice
blackberries 125g, fresh or frozen
milk to glaze
golden granulated sugar 2 tbsp to finish
cream or ice cream to serve

■ To make the pastry, tip the flour into a large bowl, add the butter and rub it in using your fingertips until the mixture resembles fine breadcrumbs. Add the icing sugar and mix well. Beat together the egg yolk and cold water and mix into the pastry using a knife. Knead together lightly, flatten into a disc, cover with clingfilm and chill for 30 minutes.

■ Tip the apples into a pan with the caster sugar, a knob of butter and the lemon juice. Cover and cook for about 10–15 minutes until tender. Add the blackberries and cook for 5 minutes. Cool.

■ On a lightly floured worksurface, roll out the pastry no thicker than a £1 coin, stamp out 12 discs and use to line a 12-hole jam tart tin. Stamp out 12 slightly smaller discs for the lids. Divide the fruit mixture between the pastry bottoms.

■ Brush the edges with a little milk and cover with the lids, pressing the edges together to seal. Crimp the pie edges with a fork and cut a small cross in the top. Brush with milk and sprinkle with granulated sugar. Heat the oven to 190C/fan 170C/gas 5.

■ Bake for about 25 minutes until golden. Cool in the tin for 5 minutes and then serve warm with cream or ice cream.

Lemon meringue pies

30 minutes + chilling ■ Makes 8

sweet or **shortcrust pastry** 500g block
unsalted butter 75g, diced and chilled
icing sugar 1 tbsp
egg 1 yolk
LEMON CURD
eggs 3, 2 whole plus 1 yolk
unsalted butter 75g, diced
caster sugar 100g
unwaxed lemons 2, zested and juiced
MERINGUE
eggs 2 whites
caster sugar 50g

■ Divide the pastry into 8. Roll out on a floured worksurface to £1 coin thickness, then stamp out a 10cm disc from each. Carefully press the pastry discs into small brioche or muffin tins and prick the bases with a fork. Chill for 15 minutes.

■ Heat the oven to 180C/160C/gas 4. Line each pastry case with a foil square and baking beans or rice. Cook for 20 minutes.

■ To make the lemon curd, beat the eggs and egg yolk together in a heatproof bowl. Add the butter, caster sugar and lemon juice. Put the bowl over (not in) a pan of simmering water. Stir until the mix is the consistency of very thick custard. Take off the heat, strain into a clean bowl and add the lemon zest. Cover the surface of the lemon curd with clingfilm, then cool. Fill each pastry case with curd. Chill for 20 minutes. Turn up the oven to 230C/fan 210C/gas 8.

■ For the meringue, whisk the egg whites until they just hold stiff peaks. Gradually add the caster sugar, beating, until the meringue is stiff and glossy. Fill a piping bag with the meringue and pipe a generous swirl of meringue over the lemon curd (or just spoon it on top). Cook for 2–3 minutes or until the meringue is tinged golden brown at the edges. Cool before serving.

Mini iced Bakewells

1 hour 15 minutes + cooling ■ Makes 12

shortcrust pastry 375g pack

raspberry jam 4 tbsp

flaked almonds 50g

apricot jam 1 tbsp, sieved

icing sugar 4 tbsp

pink food colouring

FRANGIPANE

unsalted butter 200g, at room temperature

golden caster sugar 220g

eggs 2, lightly beaten

lemon 1, zested

vanilla extract 1 tsp

ground almonds 220g

plain flour 2 tbsp

■ Roll the pastry to the thickness of a 20p coin and use it to line 12 small tart tins. Trim level with the top of the tin and chill.

■ For the frangipane, beat the butter and sugar together until light and fluffy, beat in the eggs, lemon zest and vanilla a little at a time. Fold in the almonds and flour in one go.

■ Heat the oven to 180C/fan 160C/gas 4. Spread 1 tsp raspberry jam in each base, then fill with frangipane to the top of the pastry and level off. Scatter or arrange flaked almonds over half of each tart. Bake for 25–30 minutes or until the tops are golden and springy. Leave to cool in the tin.

■ While the tarts are still warm, brush the almond-covered halves with a little apricot jam. Mix 4 tbsp icing sugar with enough water to make a spreadable icing and add enough colour to make it pale pink. Ice the non-almond halves and leave to set.

Hazelnut tartlets with white chocolate and strawberries

1 hour + chilling ■ Makes 24

plain flour 180g

icing sugar 60g

chopped hazelnuts 1 tbsp

butter 90g, chilled and diced

egg 1

FILLING

double cream 150ml

white chocolate 200g, chopped

small strawberries 12, halved

■ Put the flour, sugar and hazelnuts in to the food processor with a pinch of salt. Add the butter and process to fine breadcrumbs. With the processor running, add the egg and whizz until the dough forms a ball. You may need to add a splash of cold water if it doesn't come together quickly.

■ Roll the dough out thinly on a floured worksurface. Use a pastry cutter to cut 24 small circles about 8cm across. Press each into a mini muffin tin and put in the freezer for 20 minutes.

■ Heat the oven to 180C/fan 160C /gas 4. Bake the tart cases for 15 minutes. Meanwhile, heat the double cream in a heatproof bowl set over simmering water. Add the chopped chocolate and whisk constantly until incorporated. Spoon into the cooled pastries. Chill for an hour and then top each tartlet with a strawberry half.

Gooseberry meringue pie

1 hour 30 minutes ■ Serves 8

shortcrust pastry 375g

golden caster sugar 50g

gooseberries 400g, topped and tailed

elderflower cordial 2 tbsp

cornflour 2 tbsp

eggs 3 yolks

butter 75g, at room temperature

MERINGUE

eggs 3 whites

golden caster sugar 175g

■ Heat the oven to 200C/fan 180C/gas 6. Line a 22cm pie dish or tart tin with the pastry and bake blind for about 20 minutes or until the pastry is crisp and lightly browned. Turn the oven down to 150C/fan 130C/gas 2.

■ Put the caster sugar, gooseberries and 275ml water in a pan and bring to a simmer for 5 minutes until the gooseberries are just soft (you can add more sugar at this point). Stir in the cordial. Drain the liquid into a small pan and use 2 tbsp of it to make a paste with the cornflour, then return to the rest of the liquid, stirring to dissolve. Bring to a simmer and stir until it thickens. Beat in the yolks and butter and stir in the gooseberries. Pour into the tart case.

■ Beat the egg whites until stiff then beat in the sugar in 2 batches. Pipe or spoon the meringue onto the pie and bake for 40 minutes or until lightly browned and crisp.

Raspberry lime curd tart

1 hour ■ Serves 8

shortcrust pastry 350g

plain flour 2 tbsp

egg yolks 3

caster sugar 125g

unsalted butter 50g, melted

half-fat crème fraîche 250ml

lime 1, zested and juiced

raspberries 150g

■ Heat the oven to 200C/fan 180C/gas 6. Roll the pastry out on a floured surface to ½cm thick and use to line a 23cm loose-bottomed tart tin. Line with baking parchment and baking beans or dried beans and blind-bake for 10 minutes. Remove the baking parchment and bake for 5 more minutes or until the pastry looks dry and lightly golden. Turn the oven down to 180C/fan 160C/gas 4.

■ Whisk the egg yolks, sugar, melted butter, crème fraîche, flour, lime zest and juice together in a bowl with a pinch of salt and pour into the pastry case.

■ Sprinkle the raspberries over and cook for 30–40 minutes, or until the filling is just set. Allow to cool completely on a wire rack and serve at room temperature or chilled with cream or ice cream.

Mixed berry shortcake tart

1 hour ■ Serves 8

SHORTCAKE PASTRY

plain flour 125g

caster sugar 4 tbsp

semolina 100g

unsalted butter 125g, cold and diced

egg 2 yolks

vanilla extract 1 tsp

FILLING

double cream 284ml carton

mascarpone 250g

vanilla pod 1

caster sugar 75g

lemon curd 4 tbsp

strawberries 500g, hulled

blackberries 450g

icing sugar 1 tbsp

■ Heat the oven to 180C/fan 160C/gas 4. To make the shortcake pastry, put the flour, sugar, semolina, butter and a pinch of salt into the food processor and whizz to breadcrumbs. Add the egg yolks and vanilla extract and whizz again for no more than 30 seconds, until the shortbread mixture starts to come together.

■ Tip into a bowl and knead lightly to ensure that the mixture is thoroughly combined. Use to line a 23cm fluted tart tin. Bake for 15 minutes until golden. Remove from the oven and cool. Transfer to a serving plate.

■ To make the filling, whisk together the cream and mascarpone until smooth. Split the vanilla pod in half and, using the point of a small knife, scrape the seeds into the cream mixture. Add the caster sugar and lemon curd and mix until smooth. Spread the filling over the shortcake base.

■ Arrange the strawberries and blackberries over the cream mixture, dust with icing sugar and serve.

Peach and redcurrant lattice

1 hour 15 minutes + chilling ■ Serves 8

sweet pastry 500g

ground almonds 2 tbsp

ripe peaches 6, stoned and cut into eighths

redcurrants 200g, picked off their stalks

caster sugar 4 tbsp

lemon ½, juiced and zested

milk 2 tbsp

ground cinnamon ½ tsp

■ Roll two-thirds of the pastry out to the thickness of a £1 coin, line a 20 x 30cm fluted tart tin with it, scatter the base with ground almonds and chill for 20 minutes.

■ Heat the oven to 180C/fan 160C/gas 4 and put in a baking sheet.

■ Put the peaches, redcurrants, 3 tbsp caster sugar, lemon zest and juice in a bowl and mix. Arrange the fruit in the pastry shell over the ground almonds.

■ Roll the remaining pastry out on a lightly floured worksurface and cut into strips about 1–1½cm wide. Arrange the pastry strips over the fruit in a lattice pattern. Brush the edges of the tart shell with milk to seal. Mix the remaining caster sugar with the cinnamon. Brush the lattice strips with milk and scatter over the cinnamon sugar.

■ Bake for about 30 minutes until the pastry is golden brown and the fruit is tender. Serve with vanilla ice cream, crème fraîche or cream.

Raspberry and coconut macaroon tarts

1 hour 10 minutes + chilling ■ Makes 8

sweet pastry 350g
FILLING
egg 1, separated
caster sugar 50g
vanilla extract 1 tsp
plain flour 25g
desiccated coconut 75g
raspberry jam 4 tsp
raspberries 16
TO DECORATE
fresh coconut ¼
raspberries
icing sugar

■ Roll the pastry out on a lightly floured worksurface and use to line 8 mini brioche tins or small, fluted tartlet tins. Prick the bases and chill for 20 minutes.

■ Heat the oven to 180C/fan 160C/gas 4. Line each tin with a small square of foil and fill with baking beans and blind-bake on a baking sheet for 10 minutes, until pale golden. Remove the foil and baking beans and cook for 3 minutes.

■ To make the filling, whisk the egg yolk, caster sugar and vanilla extract. Mix in the flour and desiccated coconut. Whisk the egg white to firm peaks and stir into the mixture. Spread ½ tsp raspberry jam into each tart shell, add 2 raspberries and divide the coconut filling between the tins. Bake for 15 minutes until golden.

■ To make the toasted coconut shavings, pare thin strips using a vegetable peeler. Put on a parchment-lined baking sheet in a single layer and toast in the oven for about 5 minutes until tinged golden at the edges. Garnish with fresh raspberries, toasted coconut shavings and a dusting of icing sugar.

Pear tart

1 hour 10 minutes ■ Serves 6

golden caster sugar 200g
pears 3, halved and cored
sweet shortcrust pastry 500g
marzipan 1 block
unrefined demerara sugar 3 tbsp

■ Heat the oven to 200C/fan 180C/gas 6. Put the sugar in a pan with 400ml water. Heat until dissolved, then slip in the pears and poach for 5–10 minutes until just tender, drain and cool.

■ Roll the pastry out to the thickness of a 20p and use to line an 18cm round tart tin (or you can use a rectangular tin approximately 12 x 30cm). Bake blind for 15 minutes then take out the foil and beans and cook for a further 5 minutes, or until there are no raw patches left. Leave to cool for a few minutes.

■ Roll the marzipan out to £1 coin thickness then cut a shape so it roughly fits the bottom of the tart tin (patch in any gaps with extra marzipan). Put the pears cut-side down on the marzipan, making sure they are spaced evenly. Sprinkle over the demerara sugar and bake for 25–30 minutes or until the pears are cooked through and the marzipan has browned and puffed up. Serve in slices with double cream or custard.

Fig and almond tart

1 hour 20 minutes + chilling ■ Serves 8

puff pastry 350g

double cream 1 tbsp

egg 1 yolk

blanched almonds 125g

caster sugar 75g

unsalted butter 50g, softened

egg 1

unwaxed lemon 1, zested

ripe figs 6–8, washed and dried

apricot jam 2 tbsp

■ Roll the pastry out on a lightly floured worksurface into a rectangle about 34 x 18cm. Beat the double cream and egg yolk together and use to brush the edges of the pastry. Fold the edges of the pastry over to make a 1cm-wide border. Brush with more of the glaze and chill the pastry on a baking sheet for at least 30 minutes.

■ Heat the oven to 200C/fan 180C/gas 6. Spread the almonds on a baking sheet and toast for 6 minutes or until pale golden. Cool. Put a baking sheet in the oven.

■ Whizz the toasted almonds in a food processor until finely ground. Add the caster sugar, softened butter, egg, lemon zest and a pinch of salt. Whizz again until smooth. Spread the almond filling over the bottom of the pastry and chill for 10 minutes while you prepare the figs.

■ Cut each fig into quarters through the stalk. Arrange the figs cut-side up over the almond mixture. Slide the baking sheet onto the hot baking sheet in the oven and cook the tart for about 35–45 minutes until golden. Brush with warmed apricot jam to glaze then serve warm with crème fraîche or vanilla ice cream.

Caramelised lemon tart

1 hour 30 minutes + chilling ■ Serves 8

PASTRY

plain flour 150g, plus extra for rolling out pastry

unsalted butter 75g, cold and diced

caster sugar 1 tbsp

egg 1 yolk mixed with 2 tbsp cold water

FILLING

eggs 6

caster sugar 225g

unwaxed lemons 4, zested and juiced

double cream 250ml

icing sugar 1–2 tbsp

■ To make the pastry, put the flour, butter, caster sugar and a pinch of salt into the food processor and pulse to breadcrumbs. Add the egg mix and pulse again until the pastry begins to come together. Flatten the pastry into a disc, cover with clingfilm and chill for 1 hour.

■ Roll the pastry out and use to line a 20 x 4cm tart tin. Prick the pastry base with a fork and chill for 20 minutes.

■ Heat the oven to 180C/fan 160C/gas 4 and put in a baking sheet. Line the tart shell with baking parchment and beans and blind-bake on the baking sheet for 15–20 minutes or until pale golden. Take out the paper and beans and cook for 4–5 minutes. Cool. Turn the oven down to 150C/fan 130C/gas 2.

■ To make the filling, whisk the eggs, sugar and lemon juice until smooth. Strain through a sieve then add the lemon zest and cream and whisk again. Pour the mixture into the case, slide back in the oven and cook for 30–35 minutes or until the filling is set. Cool completely in the tin.

■ Just before serving, dust the top of the tart with icing sugar and caramelise using a blowtorch. Serve with crème fraîche or cream.

Mini chocolate pithiviers

55 minutes + chilling ■ Makes 4

....

70% dark chocolate 50g, roughly chopped
blanched almonds 100g
golden caster sugar 100g
cocoa powder 1 tbsp
butter 100g, softened
egg yolks 3, 1 whisked with 1 tbsp water
to glaze
dark rum 1 tbsp
ready-rolled puff pastry 2 x 375g packs

■ Heat the oven to 200C/fan 180C/gas 6. To make the filling, whizz the chocolate, almonds, sugar and cocoa powder together in a food processor until you have a fine crumb mixture. Add the butter, 3 egg yolks and rum and whizz a bit more to make a paste.

■ Cut 8 circles from the pastry about 9cm diameter (cut around a plate). Divide the almond paste between 4 of the circles, heaping it into the middles and leaving a 1cm border around the edges. Brush the pastry borders with the whisked egg yolk mixed with water, then drape the other 4 circles over the tops, smoothing them down over the filling.

■ Press and crimp the edges to seal, score the tops lightly in a spiral pattern with a knife, and brush all over with the remaining whisked egg yolk. Chill for 10 minutes, then bake for 20–25 minutes until puffed and golden.

Plum tart

1 hour ■ Serves 8

shortcrust pastry 500g
ground almonds 100g
eggs 5
single cream 142ml carton
butter 100g, melted
golden caster sugar 150g
plums 6–15 depending on size, halved
and stoned
unrefined demerara sugar 2 tbsp

■ Roll the pastry out to the thickness of a
£1 coin and line a 23cm loose-bottomed tart
tin. Chill for 30 minutes. Heat the oven to
180C/fan 160C/gas 4.

■ Line the pastry case with parchment,
cover with beans and bake for 15 minutes.
Lift out the beans and parchment and bake
for 5 minutes.

■ Whisk the almonds, eggs, cream, butter
and sugar until smooth and pour into the
pastry case.

■ Arrange the plums in the case cut-side
down, pushing them into the custard mixture,
they should fit fairly close together. Sprinkle
the top with demerara sugar and bake for
25–30 minutes or until the filling is set and
the plums are cooked.

Banoffee pie

40 minutes + chilling ■ Serves 10

oaty biscuits 300g

butter 60g, melted

Nestlé Carnation Caramel 397g tin

bananas 3 large, sliced

double cream 350ml

icing sugar 1 tbsp

dark chocolate 100g

■ Heat the oven to 180C/fan 160C/gas 4. Crush the biscuits in a food processor then add the melted butter and pulse to combine. Press the mixture into a loose-bottomed 24cm tart tin, in an even layer. Transfer the tin to a baking sheet and cook for 10–12 minutes, until lightly toasted and set. Leave to cool then gently release from the tin and put on a serving plate.

■ Spread the caramel over the biscuit base and chill for 1 hour. Arrange the banana slices over the toffee. Whip the cream and sugar together to form soft peaks and spread over the bananas. Melt the chocolate in a microwave or in a bowl set over a pan of simmering water. Allow to cool slightly, before drizzling over the cream.

Spiced sugar crust apple pies

45 minutes ■ Serves 4

apples 500g, peeled and sliced
caster sugar 1 tbsp
allspice ½ tsp
sweet pastry 375g sheet, cut into 1cm strips
egg 1 yolk, beaten with 1 tbsp milk
demerara sugar 2 tbsp

■ Heat the oven to 190C/fan 170C/gas 5. Toss the apples, caster sugar and allspice together. Divide the apple mixture among 4 individual ovenproof pie dishes.

■ Use the pastry strips to make a lattice on each pie and glaze with the egg mix. Bake for 20–30 minutes until golden and crisp (sprinkle a little demerara sugar over for the last 5 minutes of cooking).

Lemon and almond tarts

1 hour ■ Makes 6

ready-made sweet pastry 350g

butter 100g, at room temperature

golden caster sugar 100g

lemons 2, zested

eggs 2

ground almonds 75g

plain flour 25g

lemon curd 6 tbsp

flaked almonds 25g

icing sugar for dusting

cream or **crème fraîche** to serve (optional)

■ Heat the oven to 200C/fan 180C/gas 6. Line six 10 x 2cm loose-bottomed tartlet tins with the pastry, trim any excess and chill.

■ To make the frangipane, beat the butter, sugar and zest until creamy. Add the eggs one by one with a spoonful of the ground almonds. Mix in the remaining ground almonds and flour.

■ Spread lemon curd over the tart bases and spoon the frangipane on top. Scatter over the flaked almonds, sit on a baking tray and bake for 25–30 minutes or until the sponge is golden and puffed. Remove from the tins. Dust with icing sugar and serve warm with cream if you like.

Pineapple treacle tart with cinnamon pastry and star anise

1 hour + chilling ■ Serves 6

shortcrust pastry 250g (half a pack)

ground cinnamon 1 tsp

demerara sugar 2 tbsp

pineapple 1 small

golden syrup 200ml

fresh white breadcrumbs 120g

lemon 1, zest only, grated

star anise 3 whole ones

■ Heat the oven to 200C/fan 180C/gas 6. Put in a baking sheet to heat. Roll out the pastry to make a rectangle roughly 25 x 50cm in size. Sprinkle the cinnamon and 1 tbsp of demerara sugar over one half, then fold in half to make a square. Roll once to press it together, then use it to line a 20cm loose-bottomed tart tin or a tart ring. Chill for 15 minutes.

■ Peel the pineapple, cut into finger-thick slices, halve each piece and cut out the tough core. Catch the juice in a bowl. Measure the golden syrup into a heatproof jug and heat for 30 seconds in the microwave to thin it.

■ Stir in the breadcrumbs and lemon zest, together with 1 tbsp of pineapple juice. Pour into the lined tin. Arrange the pineapple slices on top of the treacle mixture.

■ Scatter the remaining sugar over the pineapple and dot the star anise over the tart. Put the tart on the hot baking sheet and bake for about 30 minutes until lightly browned.

Index

Picture and recipe credits

BBC Books and **olive** magazine would like to thank the following for providing photographs. While every effort has been made to trace and acknowledge all photographers, we would like to apologize should there be any errors or omissions.

Peter Campbell p27, p79, p103; Peter Cassidy p17, p21, p71, p115, p147, p209; Jean Cazals p49, p53, p67, p69, p77, p85, p89, p97, p141, p169, p171, p183; Dan Duchars p13, p87, p105; Gus Filgate p31, p33, p39, p41, p43, p73, p75, p83, p93, p99, p107, p111, p113, p123, p129, p133, p153, p167, p177, p179, p187, p211; Lisa Linder p29, p127;

Gareth Morgans p131; David Munns p91, p95, p101; Noel Murphy p15; Myles New p23, p51, p57, p59, p61, p63, p65, p189, p191, p193, p197, p199; Martin Thompson p25; Debi Treloar p35; Simon Walton p6, p19, p37, p125, p139, p165, p181, p195, p207; Philip Webb p11, p45, p55, p81, p109, p117, p119, p121, p135, p137, p143, p145, p149, p151, p155, p159, p161, p163, p172, p175, p185, p201, p203, p205; Simon Wheeler p47, p157

All the recipes in this book have been created by the editorial team at **olive** magazine.